P

BACKWARDS and BACKWARDS Guidebook

"*BACKWARDS* is deftly written and researched, and highly recommended."—**Midwest Book Review**

"A strong choice for those looking for answers about life, the universe, and everything."—**Midwest Book Review**

"Consistent with works such as *Conversations with God* and *A Course in Miracles, Backwards* clarifies and simplifies the complexities that we tend to manifest into our lives."—**TCM Reviews**

"Nanci went farther than most NDErs. ... She looked at life, and death, from multidimensional perspectives—the human, the soul, the Light Being, and Source. ... If you read just one new book about NDEs this year, make it this one."—**Vital Signs Magazine**

"Danison's elaborate but very readable story is summarized in her first book, '*Backwards: Returning to Our Source for Answers.*' ... It's a pretty tough observation, which to me lends credibility: Danison is just telling us what she learned—no sugar-coating."—**The Spokane Spokesman-Review**

BACKWARDS Beliefs

"The author sets out to compare the spiritual truths she learned during the experience with ideas from organized religion. ... Readers interested in near-death experiences may find the book compelling for its depiction of reality."—**Kirkus Book Reviews**

"What a fascinating and disturbing book (in a good way)." **Editor, FATE Magazine**

Answers From The Afterlife

"Nanci Danison's writing is crystal clear. I have zero doubt she experienced everything she wrote about in this book."—**Avleria Gangas on Amazon.com**

"An excellent book with every question answered so eloquently. Nanci's explanations and descriptions of the afterlife, in all her books, are the best I've come across in this subject. I thank God (Source) it happened to a lawyer, she can, and does, explain the unexplainable."–**Hideko Imanishi on Amazon.com**

"Incredible! Nanci L. Danison has once again bestowed upon humanity a spiritual masterpiece. Her latest book, *Answers From The Afterlife*, expounds upon much information that can be found in her three previous books. Anyone truly interested in near-death experiences, the afterlife, and creation itself, you need not look any further."—**Alex Turner on Amazon.com**

CREATE A NEW REALITY

Also by Nanci L. Danison

Books

BACKWARDS: Returning to Our Source for Answers
BACKWARDS Guidebook
BACKWARDS Beliefs: Revealing Eternal Truths Hidden in Religions
Answers From The Afterlife

DVDs

Be Your Own Psychic
Nanci Danison Interview by Ted Henry (ABC News)
Manifesting: Creation, Not Attraction
The Meaning of Life
Nanci Danison at the Edgar Cayce A.R.E.
Our 5 Spiritual Superpowers
What Happens When We Die?

CDs

The Heart of New Age Beliefs
How to Access Universal Knowledge
How to Manifest Physical Reality
Life Plan from the Afterlife
Manifest Consciously with Unconditional Love
Manifest Healing
The Purpose of Life
Revelations
The Root of All Evil
Self-Healing
Soulless Humans

CREATE A NEW REALITY

Move Beyond Law of Attraction Theory

Nanci L. Danison

A.P. Lee & Co., Ltd., Publishers
Columbus, OH

AP Lee & Co., Ltd.
PO Box 340292
Columbus, OH 43234
"Evolving mankind, one book at a time."

First Edition: October 2018

Cover design: Karen McDiarmid
Cover photo: © Shawn Reeder Photography

Library of Congress Control Number: 2018953959
ISBN-13: 978-1-934482-38-4

Printed in Canada on 100% recycled paper

Dedication

To Ryan McCormick with my deepest and most heartfelt gratitude for all you have done for my mission

Contents

Preface

THIS BOOK IS ABOUT MANIFESTING. MANIFESTING is an innate divine power to create physical matter and reality that we have as parts of God/Source—as personalities within the infinite mind and consciousness of our Creator and God. When I use the word "we" or "us," I mean Source as it is acting through Light Beings in the afterlife or through you and me within the physical universe. I never refer to humans as "us" because I learned in the afterlife that we are not human animals; we are actually the parts of Source's self-awareness that humans call "souls." We are souls. This book is addressed to the souls incarnated into human bodies so I can tell you how powerful you are, powerful enough to create the world and life of your choice. This book explains what I learned from God/Source about how to consciously and unconsciously use manifesting to have a human life more to your liking.

The truth that we create physical reality through the spiritual phenomenon of manifesting is not an idea or theory I dreamed up one day. I am not giving you my own speculations, logic, conclusions, or insights. Nor has any of this material been channeled from spirits or copied from other authors. Rather, I offer here my memories of the information about manifesting that downloaded directly into my mind during an extensive afterlife visit following my death in 1994. All I have done is put words to the telepathic "Knowings" I received in the afterlife, in order to describe and explain manifesting in simple terms.

From chapter to chapter, I repeat key concepts that are foreign to our normal religious and spiritual belief systems because it is necessary in order to fully develop the new point I am making. Also, I have learned from personal experience that it is difficult to dislodge old thinking and beliefs without constant reminders of the new concepts.

I hope reading this book will excite you and give you the incentive you need to begin to create a new life for yourself, as I have done.

Nanci L. Danison

September 2018

Acknowledgments

SO MANY PEOPLE HAVE HELPED MAKE IT POSSIBLE for me to publish this book about manifesting, and to fulfill the final piece of the mission I undertook when I returned from life in heaven, that it would be impossible for me to thank each of them individually here. I pray each of you knows in your heart of hearts that your love and support, and medical care, have kept me going long enough to complete this manuscript. Some of the many wonderful Beings of Light on Earth who have directly contributed to this book, in addition to those mentioned on the cover, are: Ryan McCormick of Goldman and McCormack PR, the best publicist in the world and host of *The Outer Limits of Inner Truth* radio show on the Internet, www.outerlimitsradio.com, and Jennifer Smith of the Cincinnati chapter of the International Association for Near-Death Studies, both of whom read a draft of the manuscript and gave me ideas for making it even better; Michele Fry, who gave me the idea for the book title in response to my request to my eNewsletter subscribers for help; and especially my beloved readers, eNewsletter subscribers, and YouTube channel viewers, who have asked me so many of the questions that fueled the content of this book.

CREATE A NEW REALITY

Move Beyond Law of Attraction Theory

1

What Is Reality?

ALL OF OUR BELIEFS ABOUT LIFE—RELIGIOUS, SPIRItual, philosophical, or scientific—spring from the central premise that we[1] are separate beings from our Creator, from our God. Everything we think we know about the universe, life, death, and the afterlife hinges on the belief that we are separate from God and have to find our way to heaven or paradise on our own. We feel alone—physically cut off from all other beings as well as our God. No matter how much we love our families and friends, we still feel as if we are separate beings from them. We feel we are individual humans cast out into life to find our own way. This is the sometimes hopeless reality many of us know.

But what if that central premise is false? What if it is not true that we are separate from our Creator, from each other, from the rest of the universe? What if we are not even human? I learned in the afterlife that the core doctrine of my childhood religion is false. We are not alone. We are not separate. And we are not left to fend for ourselves. The eternal reality I both learned and lived is that we are in truth the God we worship. That truth opened up for me a whole new world of superpowers, one of which is our power to create what humans know as physical matter. We souls can individually and collectively change the physical reality we experience as human life. Let us start with my memories of the Creation of the universe to understand how this is possible.

A Brief Summary of Creation

Before I died, I essentially believed the Genesis account of Creation—that God created the physical universe and then created me and all other humans, each possessed of an eternal soul. I wholly and completely believed I was a human being, that human life is real, and that Nanci's life was my only chance to earn my way into heaven. I found out in the afterlife that what my former religion teaches is not true. I learned that religions are based on human thinking that we souls have no reason to reject because while on earth we believe human perceptions define reality.

I learned in heaven directly from God, what I now call Source, that Source uses thought Energy to create the dream or fiction that humans experience as physical reality. The process is called "manifesting." Source's immense core consciousness imagines and mentally projects the physical universe that humans believe is real. The concept reminds me of the movie *The Matrix,* though what Source does is infinitely more sophisticated.[2] I personally watched and relived Source's memories of expelling vast quantities of mental Energy into what humans call outer space but is, in fact, part of Source's infinite mind. Over eons, Source's thought Energy eventually formed galaxies, stars, planets, clouds of gases, and everything else the wonderful Hubble telescope has brought to our viewing screens. Eons later, chemicals combined to form DNA, which then evolved into living plants and creatures, including human animals.

After creating physical matter, Source imagined zillions of personalities or characters it could play to experience physical life through the phenomenon we call incarnation. *We* are those mental personalities/characters. We are parts of Source's own consciousness and self-awareness. We are not the human bodies we occupy. They are simply vehicles Source inhabits within its imagined universe.

Near-death experiencers sometimes report seeing angel-like beings in the afterlife that they call "Beings of Light." These Beings of Light are the visual representations of Source's carefully crafted mental personalities or characters. The rest of us call Beings of Light "souls" or "spirits." In my books, I use the NDEr term *Light Beings*, or the common word *souls*, or my own term *Source's mental characters* as shorthand for Source's self-awareness in the form of its mental personalities/characters. You and I are Light Beings. We are souls. We are Source's mental characters. We are not human and we are not manifested like humans are. We exist as part of the ultimate reality of Source's consciousness. We are Source! From now on, when I say "we," I mean we Light Beings/souls, and not humans.

As miniature parts of Source, we Light Beings are the workhorses of incarnation. Like the rest of Source, we each have multiple levels of awareness that we can choose to experience collectively or individually. In addition, we each have a Source-designed unique personality composed of some traits innate to Source and some traits it can only imagine. We choose our incarnations consistent with our unique traits and reasons for experiencing physical life. To incarnate, we Light Beings follow the same process that created us: we mentally separate out part of our own Source self-awareness—one of our multiple levels of awareness—and blend it into a thing or creature in the physical universe. Humans call the part of us that incarnates the "soul." The rest of our Light Being consciousness and levels of awareness remain in what humans call heaven. The effect is similar to what you experience when you dream: part of your awareness thinks it is inside a character in the dream and part stays with the body as it sleeps. You might call this a form of bi-location. From now on, when I use the term "soul," I mean the level of Source self-awareness that each of us Light Beings has incarnated into physical matter.

When we incarnate, the physical host already exists, whether it be animal, vegetable, or mineral. In other words, a human fetus already exists before a soul incarnates into it prior to birth. Source manifested humans as a species of Earth animal with specific character traits in common with other animals. The personalities and identities we think belong to human beings are actually the eternal personalities of the Light Being souls inside them. I learned in the afterlife that human animals have their own rudimentary personalities, which are not much more sophisticated than those of domesticated dogs or horses. When part of our Light Being Energy is working as a soul, it is not part of the manifested human animal. We merely inhabit humans via incarnation, blending one level of our Light Being/ Source self-awareness intimately with theirs to the point that we are indistinguishable from our host bodies.

The incarnation process Source designed allows it to feel it is inside each and every type of physical matter into which we incarnate. The effect is similar to what we feel when we dream we are inside a dream character looking out at a dream environment and activity.

Source designed a form of amnesia that blankets us Light Being mental characters in order to give itself the sensation that what it experiences through us is real.[3] Consequently, we are presently blinded to our true nature as Source, a phenomenon that has given rise to nearly all of the misunderstandings we have about life, death, the afterlife, and everything else we care about.

Note that I do not call the physical world an elaborate illusion. It most definitely is not an illusion to humans, who experience it as their one and only reality. Yet the physical universe is not an objective, solid, set-in-stone reality that exists independent of its Creator. I learned in the afterlife that the universe exists *only* in Source's mind. The entire universe and all of its activity is Source's imagination, not unlike the computer-generated false reality in *The Matrix* or our own dreams. The physical world is Source's dream, for lack of a more accurate analogy. And we are the characters within the dream through which Source experiences the dream. We are as much part of God/ Source as our dream characters are part of us.

I watched Source create the universe out of its own thought Energy. We Light Beings likewise create physical matter and reality within the universe using Source's thought Energy. That is how we consciously and unconsciously manifest our own lives as well as the physical world we see. And, because we manifest our own physical lives, we literally have the spiritual power to create a new reality for ourselves and our human hosts!

Human Definition of Reality

Most of us believe there is only one reality—a physical, solid, shared-by-all-awake-and-aware-creatures world that we can count on being immutable. We believe this because the humans we inhabit believe it. But I learned in the afterlife that there are a million realities, the least real of which is physical life.

The bodies we inhabit believe reality must be physical, that is, something you can touch, see, smell, hear, or taste. Something a scientist can measure with an instrument. Something solid and permanent. An observation or experience that is fleeting could meet the definition of reality, but only if shared or reproducible by others.

From the human perspective, we Light Being souls seem to be part of individual physical entities called human "beings." Many recoil when I use the term *human animals*, though that is the correct biological classification. The bodies we inhabit meet the human test of reality because they occupy space, have mass, and interact with their environment. During the time we occupy human animals we souls believe we are human and that Source's dream of the universe is real.

During human life, we souls employ a weaker form of the type of imagination Source uses to manifest the universe to create our own dream characters and dreamscapes. But we believe reality exists at the level of the dreamer, the person who in waking life uses his/her bodily senses to experience the world. Humans are accustomed to accepting waking life as reality. Dreams, they are taught, are not real. Hallucinations are not real. Visions and ghostly apparitions are not real, according to human society. Imagination and creativity produce illusion, or so humans believe. Solid matter is the only reality, they think. Our human hosts' physical limitations thus restrict our sense of reality while we are inside them.

Though we Light Beings have total recall in our natural spiritual form, the parts of us invested into human bodies suffer amnesia that conceals our eternal memories and alters our sense of reality. While we experience human life, we share human beliefs. We think like humans. Feel like humans. We accept the conceit that humans are the repositories of vast storehouses of knowledge. That they know the truth: the alleged truth that physical matter is the only reality. We souls believe this because we think we have no alternative other than insanity.

Armed with the human definition of reality, we souls reject our manifestations of reality that take the form of dreams, imaginings, and creative endeavors, calling them illusions. We call them fiction. Not real. We consciously limit our sense of reality to what our animal hosts accept as real. And thus we forgot the truth about reality. The greater truth. The truth that exceeds the human capacity to understand.

I learned in the afterlife that humans are wrong about reality. Reality changes as we expand our ability to perceive it. Reality changes with our level of awareness. And there are many, many stages of awareness.

Generally, when we discuss reality we mean solid matter and shared experiences. But even at the human level of existence there are two categories, or levels, of reality: collective human reality and individual human reality. We souls and humans are familiar with dramatic changes in both.

Collective Human Reality

Most of us souls believe, because our human hosts do, that everyone sees and experiences the same Earth we do. Our photographs and videos confirm this beyond any doubt. Each of us can see the photos and watch the videos and concur that they accurately represent what we observe with our own eyes. This is proof positive. Or is it?

Anyone involved in taking witness statements, whether for court or for a government or insurance investigation, encounters the situation where the various witnesses to the same event say they saw different things. For example, Mary saw a blue SUV hit the child in the crosswalk. Joe saw a black panel van hit the child. Sally saw the child fly up into the air when struck. Max saw the little boy fall immediately to the pavement. Each witness claims the other is mistaken. Trial lawyers and scientists claim human sensory perception is unreliabile when under stress, like the stress of seeing a small child run down. Under this theory, all the witnesses may be wrong. But they are not wrong. Each witness experienced exactly what he or she describes. Our collective human reality is not as uniform as we think it is. Though we may all see a blue sky, we do not have such identical experiences when it comes to life events. What we deem to be reality changes with our perspective on it—both our physical location perspective and our mental and emotional makeup perspective.

Individual Human Reality

We have all experienced how our sense of the realities of human life changed over time as our host bodies have grown. For example, we once experienced infancy. Our entire reality centered on sleeping, being fed and burped, and having our diapers changed. We played peek-a-boo with goofy adults. Our parents carried us around in baby carriers, pushed us in strollers, and passed us off to any willing hands when we sobbed uncontrollably. We explored our body's fingers and toes as though they were foreign lands. We cooed delight at seeing our human's face peer back at us from mirrors. And we suckled pacifiers for all we were worth. That was our total individual reality then. Does all that still seem like your real life? Do you even remember any of it? Can you imagine your life being like that now? Does it seem unreal now that you once thought that infant experience was what life was all about?

We also experienced being young children. Our waking thoughts revolved around what we were going to play each day and who would be our playmates. Mom helped us dress or laid out our clothes for us. We pretended to brush our teeth and wash our hands. We bounded down the stairs to a breakfast that magically appeared on the kitchen table. Our days were spent playing ball or dressing dolls, riding bikes or taking hikes, chitchatting with our little friends, and keeping our eyes open to the wonders of the world we explored. We slept, ate, played, and possibly performed small chores to earn money for toys or candy. That was all there was to reality. Does that kind of life still seem real to you? Do you remember much of it? Can you imagine yourself living like that now and thinking it is the reality of human life?

As our bodies aged, others taught us the difference between fiction and reality. Our parents forced us early on to distinguish the two because mothers and fathers do not appreciate being told what they consider to be lies. Lies are bad, they told us. Imaginative stories are not "real," we were told. So we came to distrust our non-physical friends, whom our parents called imaginary. And we rejected our creative talents, judging them frivolous and childish because our parents did. We reined in our daydreams because we were scolded for having them. And we resolved to limit our experiences to what human society deemed to be reality.

Sadly, as adults many of us have had the painful experience of being deceived by what we totally believed was the reality of our lives. You might have believed with your whole heart that your spouse loved you unconditionally and was true to his marriage vows. When you find out your beloved cheated on you, your married life is shattered. Or, you believe your employer values you, and that you have done everything humanly possible to earn a promotion, only to watch it be awarded to someone else. Your self-confidence is shattered. Perhaps you believe our country values all races and sexes and are shocked to see a lifelong bigot and sexist elected president. Your faith in your fellow man is shattered. Obviously we did not all share the same reality in these scenarios.

The human condition also confines our sense of reality to what we *most recently* experienced. What we are doing right now seems real to us. And we find it very difficult to get back into the mindset we had at an earlier age when we thought what we were experiencing then was the reality of life. For humans, reality is a moving target with the bull's eye painted on today.

Manifested Reality

Human Life Is Real Only While We Live It

We souls have come to believe that waking human life is real while we are living it. It feels real. It smells and tastes and sounds real. We have real emotions and sensations. Our experiences are real. But when we return to the greater reality of the afterlife, and remember who and what we truly are, we easily recognize human life for the dream it is. With a change in our level of awareness comes a change in what we perceive to be reality.

When I was in the afterlife, after I had regained my memories of hundreds, even thousands of physical and nonphysical lifetimes, I was flabbergasted that I could ever have thought Nanci's life was my real life. It seemed completely absurd to me that I had once totally believed I was merely human. I knew from eternal truths implanted into my mind earlier in heaven that we live in a fog of amnesia while we inhabit physical matter, which generally prevents us from remembering who and what we truly are. And yet, while in heaven I still could not accept that I had once thought my life as Nanci the human was reality.

Instead, looking back on Nanci's life from heaven, I felt as though a part of the "complete me" that exists in the afterlife had been asleep and had dreamed Nanci's entire life. For reasons I had yet to understand, my conscious awareness on Earth had been limited to what I experienced as the dream character of Nanci. I knew I woke up from that dream by leaving human life, crossing over, and resuming my spiritual life. In a sense, this is exactly what happens.

We Light Beings do split our consciousness and awareness between the afterlife and physical life through Source's power of multiple simultaneous levels of awareness. We invest one level of our awareness into a human animal (or any other physical matter) as its soul. The rest of our consciousness, awareness, personality, and memory stays in the Light. We continue to live eternal life at the same time we experience physical life, the latter through something like a dream state. When the time is right, the manifested form we inhabit dies and the part of our Light Being awareness posing as the soul returns to recombine with the part that remained in heaven.

I learned in the afterlife that human life is real only to that part of our awareness that believes it is living a human life, the soul. How can that be? How can we split off part of our consciousness and awareness and insulate it from the truth of our greater existence? The answer lies in Source's innate ability to hold multiple simultaneous levels of awareness. As parts of Source we are capable of having more than one state of awareness at the same time. And those states may or may not connect and/or communicate with one another.

As parts of Source we are similarly capable of creating multidimensional thoughts that include our own imaginary beings. We call these thoughts dreams, daydreams, or flights of fantasy. Our dreams and imaginings are populated by personalities we create, which may or may not reflect actual people in our lives. Authors and actors also create characters that appear to be separate beings from the writer or actor. As a licensed private investigator, I occasionally created a fictitious character to play during undercover operations. Undercover police officers do the same thing. We all create characters in human dreams that appear in the dream to be separate beings from ourselves. The grand difference between our imagined or dreamed characters, and what Source is doing when it creates us, lies in our own emotional and intellectual sense of what is real.

Our perception of reality depends entirely upon whether we are suffering the amnesia of incarnation or have awakened to our true identity as Source. When I asked how all this worked, Knowings about manifesting inundated my thoughts. During my extensive time in the afterlife I received vast quantities of information in a form I call "Knowings." Knowing describes how I felt after absorbing the information; that is, I felt as though I knew the subject completely from all angles and as deeply as if I had lived it myself. More important, I *remembered* knowing the facts I received in the afterlife *before* I entered into Nanci's body. The Knowings about incarnation and amnesia explained that Source's ability to manifest physical reality accounts for these disparate levels of what seems real to us. I learned that each of us Source characters/Light Beings, and soul parts of Light Beings, has the very same ability to create what humans accept as physical reality. We *are* the Creator.

Manifested Collective Reality

Source created the physical universe for the purpose of having a context within which to experience what it is like *not* to be itself. Source wanted to experience "otherness." It wanted to have relationships that could reflect more facets of its many, many personalities. In short, Source wanted to grow. So, it fantasized, or dreamed, an environment we call the universe. Source then populated that dreamscape with beings, creatures, plants, and inanimate objects that all change over time according to evolution and/or specifications that Source designed. Only self-aware manifested creatures, like humans, believe that the universe is real. To Source the universe is just like our dreamscapes are to us.

Most of us souls believe the human theory that reality is something that exists separate and apart from us—physical matter that existed before we were born and will continue after our hosts' deaths. We souls cannot imagine how our thoughts and beliefs could possibly affect what we perceive to be the physical universe—an objective, solidified, observable physical truth. How could our paltry thoughts possibly matter in the face of all that?

Our thoughts and beliefs are all that matters. We Light Beings co-create with the core entity Source and one another the physical world humans experience. I learned in the afterlife about a group of Light Beings I call "All Those With An Interest In Earth," which includes us. Our collective co-creations form the well-known and seemingly permanent physical matter objects and creatures that populate Earth. While inside humans, we experience this default collective manifestation along with humans. Yet our individual experiences of that collective environment are unique, as we manifest them moment to moment.

You may not believe you can manifest a whole world of physical matter. Out-of-body experiencers, including many near-death experiencers (NDErs), are familiar with instantly manifesting physical environments. They have personal knowledge of the wonder and joy, and sometimes terror, of thinking something one second and seeing it in physical matter the next. As soon as we souls leave the human body we can instantly use this innate spiritual talent. And the result can be quite startling if we are not prepared for it. Moreover, unless the out-of-body soul is given Knowings that anything it expects to see can manifest into what humans believe to be physical reality, it will undoubtedly believe that it has actually visited another physical realm—or a spiritual dimension with human-like features. This is partly how stories of heaven as an actual physical place got started.

Manifested Individual Reality

The truth is this: your own physical reality is what you manifest for yourself, alone and in cooperation with other Light Beings.

Manifesting is an innate ability we Light Beings have because we are part of Source. It is our very nature. We manifest automatically. We souls each unconsciously manifest our own physical matter reality. We do it alone and by agreement with other Light Being souls. And, just as Source manifested this universe, we manifest our own individual worlds to experience—each one very similar to what our co-creators may manifest, yet very dearly our own. Our reality is invested with our unique life views, as well as our own wounded human perspectives.

An individual soul's unique beliefs and perspectives govern what that soul will manifest into the physical reality it experiences. And there are so very many perspectives available. They range from happy, carefree attitudes about life to severely damaged viewpoints, with the underlying belief systems to support them. They stem from beliefs that were formed through human experience, usually at a very young age. Beliefs that were never tested for congruence with the realities other people see. Beliefs that have never been exposed to the light of logical analysis. Beliefs that are carried silently, hoarded as though precious but toxic in their effect on manifesting. We all have toxic beliefs about ourselves and life itself that we manifest experiences to match, but some souls carry huge burdens in this regard.

For example, the part of Source's awareness inside a little boy who is emotionally abused can by force of repetition come to believe the hurtful things his emotionally damaged father says. When the person we trust the most hurts us, not only does the body take it to heart, but the soul takes is to heart as well and believes the same painful things the body feels. We are, after all, in this together—body and soul. The little boy's original perception of his life as safe and wonderful is whittled down by abuse to a world where he is unworthy of love, incapable of doing anything right, and the victim of everyone around him. In defense, the boy constructs a fantasy mental picture of himself to hold on to in order to survive emotionally. The little boy then grows into a man who paradoxically acts as though he has an overinflated opinion of himself. He bullies others because he has no empathy for them. He manipulates them. He feigns exaggerated injury from the slightest offense. And he perceives everything he does not like to be an offense directed at him, whether it has anything to do with him or not. Psychologists may label this damaged man as having narcissistic personality disorder. However, I learned from Knowings that such a label misses the point. This little boy grew into adulthood with a damaged perspective on life and himself within it and manifested events and experiences to match his beliefs.

In another situation, a little girl who grows up in a family with two alcoholic parents may fall through the cracks of their attention. Fortunately, she is not actively harmed, physically or emotionally. But she suffers abuse just the same, via neglect. This little girl, born full of love and wonder, soon starts to believe she is invisible. Her parents pay no attention to her small accomplishments. She hears no praise for doing things well. Her parents shove her aside to focus on the problem child in their lives. She starts school with a belief that she should do nothing to bring attention to herself. When she does not understand the teacher because she has a hearing problem, she tells no one and simply turns invisible. Or, because of poor vision, when she cannot interpret the writing on the board or screen, she assumes that is normal and tells no one. The invisible girl grows up to be an invisible woman who believes she is unworthy of notice, much less love. And she falls for the first man who pays her any attention, whether he treats her well or badly. The two have children that the woman largely ignores because that is the only parenting model she knows. And the cycle repeats itself. This little girl grew into adulthood with a skewed perspective on life and her role in it and manifested events and experiences to match her beliefs.

Far less toxic beliefs held by emotionally healthy humans can still cause devastating manifestations. Think of the man who has never been told he is attractive and so manifests a life full of appearance and behavior choices that make him unattractive, resulting in few successful interactions with the opposite sex. Compare him with the man who is objectively no more attractive, but who believes he is God's gift to women and so makes more pleasing appearance choices and manifests opportunities to boost his self-confidence with women. A woman who has been treated like her looks are her only asset may believe she is a dumb blonde and may manifest situations that reinforce that belief. Someone who believes everyone lies will be lied to repeatedly. A woman who believes every man cheats on his wife will be cheated on. A man who believes rich men get all the breaks will manifest fewer opportunities to be successful himself. Our human lives can become vicious cycles simply because we manifest into physical reality beliefs that do not serve us well.

Regardless of where we are physically and mentally, our manifestations are reality—for us. Whether physical or non-physical, solid or ephemeral, shared by others or reserved for our private enjoyment, our manifestations are real experiences. Dreams are reality. Daydreams are reality. Artistic creations are reality. Nightmares are reality. Drug-induced hallucinations are reality. Characters we construct from fiction are reality. Everything we manifest to experience is reality—to us and no one else.

Reality is whatever we manifest to experience. Experience is reality, for the reason we were created is to have experiences for Source that are believable—this is the truth about manifested reality.

One of my readers, understandably mired in the belief that humans are real, tried to pin me down on which human behaviors are manifested and which result from independent human action. The answer is there are no independent human acts. Humans, including their biology and character traits, are manifested by the core entity Source. Human animal behaviors, such as eating, drinking, sleeping, nesting, recreating, and procreating, are part of the biology Source manifested into them. All other human experiences are consciously or unconsciously manifested by the Light Being soul inside the body, alone or together with other Light Beings by agreement. In sum, from all perspectives other than the human one, nothing about human life is real. So we souls can change it!

Spiritual Reality

In the same way that our own infancy and early childhood seem unreal to us now, our entire human lives will seem unreal to us once we leave them behind for the afterlife. We will have total recall of everything that happened to us on Earth. But human life will feel like a dream in comparison to how much more real the afterlife is.

For a short while, we may manifest physical reality in heaven. We are so used to doing it that it has become habit. And, because we can instantly manifest physical matter environments in heaven, we find it exciting to immediately enjoy the fruits of our manifesting powers. This is why some NDErs see beautiful gardens or crystal cities, hear ethereal music, and see being-like apparitions that look like angels or religious figures. Eventually, though, every soul acclimates to spiritual life as it recombines with the rest of its Light Being Energy that remained in heaven during the soul part's incarnation. Each soul undergoes an intellectual and emotional transformation back to its natural, spiritual self. Then, the afterlife becomes its sole reality and everything outside the afterlife feels like fiction.

Ultimate Reality

There is only one ultimate reality: Source. The buck stops there. Everything short of full awakening to our true identity as Source seems illusory in comparison to the ultimate reality of Source's existence.

Source imagined everything humans perceive as the universe, but these imaginings are not real to Source. Hence, they are not ultimate reality. Physical manifestations do not automatically have what we call soul. Source has to choose to inhabit something in the physical world in order for it to have a soul. So, in a sense, physical matter is a thought, dreamscape, or mental framework for Source's mental characters to delve into and invest with Source's awareness. Right now, some of us souls have chosen to inhabit human manifestations.

We Light Beings/souls are real because we are part of Source's consciousness and Source is ultimate reality. Yet, we exist solely in the mind of Source. From Source's perspective, we are unique facets of its own self-awareness, and we exist now and forever within Source's mind and imaginings. We are not separate. We are not beings. We are not physical. Yet, we are real. We are creative expressions of an overwhelming, unconditional self-love—the truest reality about Source. We are Source experiencing its love for itself. Love is our ultimate reality.

Because Source is ultimate reality, and everything else is its imagination, we parts of Source's mind can use our imagination and manifesting superpower to create a new reality for ourselves. The following chapters will explain in detail how.

Important Takeaways from Chapter 1

- I learned in heaven, directly from God/Source, that we are not humans, which are manifested Earth animals. Rather, the personalities and consciousness we identify as ourselves are actually subpersonalities/mental characters within Source's infinite mind (like book characters in an author's mind). I call us Light Beings, but we are still Source. We inhabit humans and other physical matter as their souls.

- We souls incarnate as Source's way of living inside physical matter creatures and things and experiencing physical life in its many forms from the inside. It is similar to how we experience our own dreams at night from inside a dream character version of ourselves.

- Knowings I received in heaven explained that physical reality is manifested, created, by Source via its thoughts and imagination. As parts of Source's consciousness, we souls have the very same ability to create physical reality. So, we souls can change the human lives we experience by consciously manifesting something new or different.

- Reality is pliable and changes as we expand our ability to perceive it, as well as when our perspective changes through age, experience, or spiritual transformation. Each of us Light Being souls, individually and in concert with other Light Beings, manifests what we individually experience as human life. Because we manifest life ourselves, we can change it.

- The ultimate reality is our Creator, the Source of all life.

2

Afterlife Lessons in Manifesting

I LEARNED HOW TO CONSCIOUSLY CREATE PHYSICAL reality the hard way: I died. And I entered the vastly more wonderful and expansive reality of our Creator, what I call Source. I share with you now the Knowings I was given about how physical matter and physical life is created.

I Learned About Manifesting in Heaven

I learned about *manifesting*—creating physical matter—at three different stages of my first afterlife visit. The information is so important that it was repeated three times in different ways to make sure I fully understand it. At the time, I had no idea why it was so important. The impression I got was that the Light Being souls inside humans had unknowingly adopted a human interpretation of manifesting that Source wanted to correct. I later learned I was to be the messenger of this correction.

I entered the afterlife for an extended stay after I died during an invasive medical procedure. Using mammograms for guidance, a radiologist inserted a wire into my breast to mark three tumors for surgical biopsy on March 14, 1994. I did not know it then, but I am allergic to something she used. So I died from anaphylactic shock, probably compounded by the effects of very low blood sugar, as documented in my hospital record.

When I first entered the Light, wave after wave of blissful love and acceptance billowed through me, filling me with more knowledge than I could ever have imagined existed. I was gently and lovingly convinced that I am not the human being I know as Nanci. Instead, I am eternal Source Energy and consciousness completely separate from but inhabiting a human body. I was inundated with extensive Knowings about the nature of human animals, their abilities and limitations, and how they are far more like dogs and horses than the person I thought myself to be. Humans are merely manifestations—no more real than our human life dream characters. I was given to understand that the personality and identity I had always assumed to be human actually belongs to me—the Source consciousness, Light Being, and soul inside Nanci's body. The human I left behind when I died was a wonderful host, but I was told it had no more personality or character than my little dog Ginger. I actually did an inventory of my personality traits and emotions while in the Light to confirm this. I discovered I was still me without Nanci's body.

Shortly after absorbing this knowledge about my relationship to my former body, I realized that my perspective had shifted. No longer did I perceive myself the way I did while in human form. I could mentally step back and observe myself as a newly arrived soul reacquainting itself with the Light. Then I could move my point of view back farther and objectively observe myself observing myself. Again and again I expanded my point of view of myself, all the while seeing my relative importance in the grand scheme of things become smaller and smaller. Yet as the perspectives multiplied I retained all of the mental awareness of each earlier level. I had multiple simultaneous levels of awareness.

While exploring this newfound ability, I noticed a body slightly to my right and below me. I could see it through the invisible back of what felt like where my head should have been. This was the first person I saw in the afterlife. I temporarily found this being more interesting than the mental powers I had been exercising. I observed a female human with her head held high and arms resting on the arms of a chair in which she sat facing away from the door of a mammography room. Using human points of reference, I judged the room to be about one floor below me, as if I were seeing it while floating on the ceiling. Looking closer, I recognized her as Nanci, the body I had recently departed. She looked alive, but empty, devoid of spark. Her physical appearance was not at all what I remembered myself looking like in the mirror or photos. I remember thinking to myself, *Wow, I don't see what all that vanity was about. She sure doesn't look like much now.* A part of me found my attitude toward my former body offensive. Here was this wonderfully generous human being who had carried me around for forty-three years, shared every moment of her life without objection, and died so that I could come home to the afterlife. I was ashamed of myself for not feeling more compassion toward her. But I felt nothing. The body I had loved my whole life meant no more to me than the chair she was sitting in. I thought, *Body, chair, floor—it all feels the same to me emotionally.* Though I did not know it then, it *is* all the same: it is all manifested physical matter.

Experiments in Manifesting

Seeing my former body below me triggered a tiny inkling of understanding of what was going on. But I refused to believe I had died. I specifically recall telling myself: *Nah, I couldn't have died! I heard you go through a tunnel when you die and I didn't ...*

My thought was interrupted by the sudden appearance of a tunnel. But not the glorious star-filled celestial wormhole populated by loved ones that I later read about in others' near-death experience accounts. This was a dirt tunnel. Cold, smelly, dark, old. It appeared to be spanning a narrow road running beneath a train trestle—maybe in the early days of the Model T Ford. I could feel my feet firmly planted on the ground, even though I had just confirmed to myself that I no longer inhabited a physical body. I could smell wet soil and mold. Night things sang their nocturnal greetings. The air was moist and weighed heavy on my skin. The tunnel and road on which I stood felt as completely real as anything I had ever experienced while inside Nanci. But I knew for a fact that I was in the Light, not on

Earth in a tunnel. So the scene did not fool me into believing it was real. I began to suspect what was going on—that I had died—so I decided to experiment.

First experiment: I said to myself, *I've also heard it described as a beautiful meadow.* (I was not yet brave enough to admit that "it" was heaven.) Instantly, I was standing at the edge of a sun-dappled breezy meadow. Birds sang. Bees buzzed. Purple-hazed mountains dominated the distance. The air was warm and fragrant. The scene reminds me now of one in the movie *What Dreams May Come* in which Robin Williams is running through a field of oil-paint flowers. My meadow, however, looked and felt exactly as it would on Earth. Yet I knew I was not physically located on Earth anymore. I thought maybe another experiment would convince me of what I was beginning to recognize from deeply buried, ingrained memory.

Second experiment: I told myself that my visit to heaven so far had been an hallucination and that I was actually still on Earth in the hospital. Instantly, I found myself walking down an institutional hallway, inhaling the universally recognizable stale, antiseptic hospital smell. I could feel my feet solidly striking the floor and my body weight pressing down on them. I felt the wire the radiologist had inserted sticking out of my breast tenting the hospital gown I wore. Looking to my right, I saw a purple stripe painted on the wall, indicating that I was headed in the direction of the operating rooms. I sensed, rather than saw, the physical presence of a nurse beside me. Her perfume wafted over the less pleasant hospital air. Everything was absolutely as real as anything I had ever experienced while inside Nanci. Yet not even the intensity and logic of this scene could convince me that I was not still in the Light.

Mentally, I compared each of the three seemingly physical experiences with what I had believed to be reality on Earth. The tunnel, meadow, and hospital corridor were just as real as anything I had experienced encapsulated in Nanci's body. They were *real* based on all the experiences I had ever had in human life. But I knew they were *not* real because I had instantly conjured the physical environments simply by thinking them. Both could not be true. And I knew which reality was truly real: that I was in the Light, in the afterlife. I knew this in the same way we all do when we make distinctions between what is real and what is illusion in human life.

For example, I once had a nightmare that two men broke into my house and shot me point-blank in my chest while I was in bed. In the dream, I saw myself sleeping and then waking up when I heard two men walking stealthily from my house's front door to my bedroom. They were whispering very softly. I cursed myself for leaving the bedroom doors open, thereby making myself more vulnerable. I wanted to get up and run, but found myself paralyzed, frozen beneath the folds of my bedcovers. My heart was jackhammering in my chest. Terror drove sweat down my forehead and neck into my pillow. The two men walked into my bedroom, turned toward my bed, and raised their guns. I had just a moment for a final thought before death: *So this is it. I'm going to die.* I calmly accepted it and waited for the bullets to hit my chest. I did not feel them hit, so I guessed I had jumped out of my body beforehand. But I still seemed to be in my bed. Then I remembered that I had seen the men turn right at my bedroom doorway to face my bed, which would have been impossible in the real world. Holding tenaciously to that bit of reality, I convinced myself I was having a nightmare and woke up from the dream. The nightmare still seemed vividly real. I had real emotional responses to it. But I knew mentally that it could not be real because I was still alive. There were no bullet holes anywhere. I looked up at the wall beside the doors and saw that the burglar alarm had not gone off. This confirmed there had been no men breaching my home's security. I chose observable facts and logic over my bodily sensations to decide what was real and what was a dream.

We all have to make choices between perceptions in much the same way. We have to distinguish what happens in very powerful dreams from the realities of waking life. Those who have had hallucinations, natural or medication-induced, use rational thought to reject the illusion and cling to the sense of reality that sustained them before the hallucination. For example, after my mother had a massive stroke, she saw a spaceship land on a hospital roof below her window. Small aliens got out to explore the roof's features. It took a while, but my mother was able to segregate that experience into the "unreal" category because no one else saw the spaceship. My mother trusted the reality that others would have seen the spaceship had it really been there.

Using those same powers of perception and discernment while in the afterlife, I was convinced that no matter how real the tunnel, meadow, and hallway felt, they did not fool me because I knew for certain that I was in the Light. Alarmed, I thought, *Fool me? FOOL me? Physical reality could FOOL me? How did that happen?* The answer came to me in one word: *manifesting.* The Knowing that a soul in the afterlife can manufacture, or manifest, into physical form the entire world that humans know as reality lit up my mind like a million-watt bulb. I had no idea what manifesting is, or how it works, but I was certain it explained what I had always thought was my real life as the human named Nanci. And I began to suspect there was a lot more to it.

A bit later in the afterlife, I transformed from believing I was human back into my spiritual identity through a transitional process we all go through after entering the Light. This gentle enlightening process in the Light extinguishes our conviction that we are human beings. It also reorients our thinking away from human attitudes to an unconditionally loving attitude.

Knowings About Manifesting

At one point in the transition from human to Light Being perspective, my mind was crammed with Knowings about manifesting. The English word *manifesting* came into my mind as the title of the subject jamming my thoughts, though nearly every other Knowing I received in the afterlife came via wordless mental telepathy. *Manifesting* was one of the very few English words I heard during my entire afterlife visit. So I knew it must be important that I remember and understand fully what it means.

I realized that by previously creating a tunnel, meadow, and hospital corridor I had used the power of manifesting physical reality just after entering the Light, before I had accepted that I had died in the physical world. Knowings explained to me exactly how I had manifested my own thoughts/expectations into what I perceived to be physical matter and reality. I learned that because humans are manifestations, and not like the parts of Source's awareness I call Light Beings, they have very little control over their lives. Much of their daily lives and routine behaviors are the result of Source-designed human appetites, drives, and chemical processes necessary for survival.

More important, Knowings also taught me that we Light Being souls have the ability to control the non-biological aspects of the lives of the physical matter creatures and things into which we incarnate. We souls can choose either to sit back and allow our host bodies to play out their animal lives, or, to take control and engage in behaviors more to our liking. We do it by directing our bodies' actions in various situations and by consciously and unconsciously manifesting events and opportunities into our hosts' lives. In short, human life is composed of both biologically driven animal behaviors and soul-directed behaviors, events, and opportunities. And we souls can increase the frequency of our conscious manifesting by simply becoming aware of our manifesting power and exercising it more often.

I lived as a Light Being for a while, enthusiastically sampling all of Source's knowledge, what I call Universal Knowledge. I soon discovered that all I had to do to have a question answered via download of Knowings into my mind was focus my attention and intention on receiving the answer. I had no idea how long I would be able to access this Universal Knowledge. So I prioritized and asked the most crucial questions first: Who am I? Who is God? What is the purpose of life? Why was I on Earth? What does God expect of me? Where is heaven? Where is hell? What is the one true religion?[4] The answers I got were not even close to what I believed before I died—what the Catholic Church and schools had taught me. This upset me so much that I demanded to know why I could not have been told these truths during human life. I felt betrayed by my parents, schools, and religion—as though they thought I could not be trusted to handle the simple truth. To quell my anger, I was shown a documentary-style vision of the development of religions nestled within the context of Earth's entire history and future.[5]

I Witnessed the Universe Being Manifested

After the Earth history lesson, I went beyond the state we typically call heaven and evolved into a formless entity: something I can only describe as a free-floating consciousness, intelligence or personality, and others may call a spirit or Energy. I continued to experience life in this form by merging into one or more of five Light Being friends I met in the Light and who experienced my life review with me. While merged, I lived bits and pieces of their memories of the physical lives they had lived. After I became adjusted to the merging Energy experience, my friends and I moved deeper into the corona of Energy surrounding the core consciousness of Source. I ultimately reawakened to the truth that I am Source. We all are.

Moving through Source's Energy corona, while assimilating new and deeper understandings of the same Knowings I had previously received in heaven, provided me with the most complete understanding of manifesting. I was privileged to observe Source's act of manifesting the entire physical universe within its own infinite mind. I witnessed Creation! I saw and felt Source's mental Energy joyously explode into the intellectual and physical brilliance of everything in the universe. I noted with surprise that Source did not create individual planets, stars, creatures, or things as I had read in the Bible. Instead, it formulated what we call "laws of nature" that govern how physical matter behaves and impressed those laws upon the Energy it used to produce the universe in its mind. Over what humans perceive to be time, those laws operated to coalesce mental Energy into physical matter, forming larger and more complex parts of the universe we observe. Living creatures and things evolved from organic and inorganic chemicals according to the laws of biology that Source invented.

After Source manifested environments, it decided to populate the universe with creatures and things. Source's purpose is to invest its own consciousness and self-awareness into various creatures and things in order to feel what it is like to have physical existence in its many forms. Because Source is All-Knowing, it already grasped intellectually what physical life is like. But Source wants to feel physical life emotionally. It wants firsthand sensory experience. One of my book readers expresses this intent beautifully:

> To comprehend infinite consciousness, such as the Source you talk about, means it totally makes sense for it to limit itself to the confines of a physical reality where all knowledge of itself is forgotten. This allows it to experience genuine feelings in a reality where the ultimate fear is not existing. Source can imagine not existing, which is the biggest emotion we have here on Earth as we struggle with the death of people we know and eventually ourselves. Without the fear of death and not existing, we couldn't experience such powerful emotions of loss, and love. The beauty in these emotions could never be felt by something infinite.[6]

In short, Source manifested the universe in order to explore its own depth of emotions and gain the sensory experience of creatures and things that it could only imagine. Each one of us inhabiting a human as its soul is in ultimate reality Source itself experiencing the physical universe through us.

The Manifesting Message

Right before I returned to Nanci's body I had access to Source's core mind and memories of Creation and then better understood the power of manifesting. I brought that knowledge back to earth. At the time of my visit to heaven, I had never heard of manifesting in the spiritual sense. I believe one reason I have remembered so much about it is that it turned out that part of my mission back in human life is to offer the world Source's explanation of how physical reality is constructed. There is general familiarity with the idea that we can influence reality spiritually, such as through prayer. Some enlightened souls understand that Source manifested the physical universe. Few realize that the universe is composed entirely of Source's thought Energy. Most of what is written about Creation presents it from the human animal observational perspective; that is, the view we have looking up from the bottom of a conceptual model in which God/Source is separate from us and we are subservient to it. Source is portrayed as being out there in the universe somewhere, answering our prayers by sending us material goods. This model of life is the opposite of everything I learned in the afterlife.

We are not now, and never have been, separated from our Source, our Creator. We Light Being souls inside humans remain firmly fixed as subpersonalities of Source's own identity, within its self-awareness and consciousness. Likewise, humans are not separate from Source. Humans are the same type of manifestation that I created three times while I was in the Light. The same manifestations as rocks, trees, sky, and oceans, and composed of the same Source thought Energy. All of Creation exists solely within Source's mind. It merely appears to be real while we inhabit the manifested human's perspective. The belief in separation is entirely human in origin. So any explanation of manifesting that revolves around Source being a separate entity from us is of human design.

Other NDErs Learned About Manifesting

Other near-death experiencers (NDErs) also learned about manifesting while in heaven. One extensive NDE account, that of Natalie Sudman, states, "After all, from an expanded consciousness perspective, it's understood that belief—*thought*—creates reality."[7] Ms. Sudman never labels the phenomenon as manifesting, but that is what she describes in this sentence. Anita Moorjani also mentions manifesting in her NDE account posted on the website for the Seattle chapter of the International Association for Near-Death Studies:

> I was shown how illnesses start at an energetic lev-

> el before they become physical. … I was given the understanding that this applies to everything in our lives, not only illnesses but physical conditions, psychological conditions, etc. I was "shown" that everything going on in our lives was dependent on our energy that is created by ourselves. Nothing was solid—we created our surroundings, our conditions, etc., depending on where this "energy" was.[8]

Ms. Moorjani uses the term "energy" in this passage for what I call "attention and intention." The Rev. Juliet Nightingale visited the afterlife while in a coma caused by colon cancer and experienced manifesting firsthand. She writes:

> I would simply think about something and it would instantly manifest … or I'd think about a place and there I'd be! … It seemed that the point in all this was the fact that we co-create with the Light. … How auspicious it is, then, to realize that as souls we are a part of all creation and take part in the actual creative process thereof![9]

Richard L. was informed during his NDE that we manifest our own surrounding reality based on our beliefs:

> My first question was "Is this heaven?"
>
> "It can be, if that's what you want. It can be Hell as well, if that's what you believe. **This reality is an extension of you**, instantly realized and formed. You always create your own reality, no matter where you find yourself, for we are all co-creators."[10]

The most extensive discussion of Creation and manifesting in an NDE account, other than my own, appears in Mira Sai's conversation with cosmic wisdom, which is posted on the Near-Death Experience Research Foundation website:

"But if this Consciousness alone is real, the world was an illusion? Then where did it come from?"

"Like all manifestation, the world too is the creation of the great illusion or great delusion, which being the Creative aspect of this Supreme Consciousness, or the Lord, is the divine movie-projector of life, in the all-powerful play of the realm of Creation. Just as a mirage in the desert disappears when viewed from a certain perspective, your life as Arti on earth has disappeared, when viewed from the perspective of the Divine Self, where you are now.

Only the eternal is real; and from the viewpoint of that Reality, all that is non-eternal, disappears. Yet of course, you, being atman (the soul) which is eternal, can still view the 'world of illusion' if you wish."

"So my life as Arti never really existed at all, it was an illusion?"

"Oh, it existed; just as a dream exists, or a movie, or a mirage."

"So the world, was just a figment of my imagination? How did I create it? With my thoughts and desires?"

"Y e s s s s!"

The answer seemed to echo all around and reverberated within my being. Yes … I understood now. The world had all been only in my mind, a thought-and-senses created illusion/delusion. Without the senses, mind and body, there was now no "ego" to perceive the world illusion!

It had all existed and happened in my mind!

Our true reality exists outside of the mind, which is where I was at the present moment.[11]

Near-death experiencer Guenter Wagner's account says this about manifesting:

> When Guenter Wagner responded that he did not know how, the beings manifested a beautiful, flower-filled meadow for him to play in. Guenter recognized the meadow as a mere manifestation, saying: "I knew that it was only an image of a meadow, somehow conjured up and suspended in this new world."[12]

NDE researcher and author P.M.H. Atwater described a scene she manifested in the afterlife while relating her NDE to an audience at the Edgar Cayce Institute in Virginia Beach. She constructed a house in heaven, thought-by-thought, until it was as real and solid as the physical matter on earth. She realized that her thoughts were creating the physical matter of the house, though she did not call the process manifesting. And NDEr Christian Andreason explained manifesting this way:

> If you think it, it can be done. What many of us fail to realize is that each of us DOES have the ability to manifest any visualization into material form. In Heaven, because all things are made from the essence of pure LIGHT, this process is done much easier. In Heaven, we have the ability to sculpt density into the Light (using concentration) and this is how we create form throughout the Realm. We do this by lightly focusing (or pressing) with our intention.[13]

It may not seem so remarkable to you that NDErs manifest earthly scenes in heaven for, after all, they are operating as spiritual beings there. A more remarkable Knowing I received in the afterlife is that we Light Being souls also manifest physical reality *while inside human bodies!*

In order to truly understand manifesting, and deliberately employ it in your life, you will have to set aside lifelong beliefs and open your mind to a new way of thinking. This book is designed to help you do that.

Important Takeaways from Chapter 2

- I learned about manifesting directly from Source/God/the Creator while in the afterlife, not from channeling anyone in the afterlife, from reading books, or creating my own theories. I received Knowings about manifesting three different times, the last of which while I was merged into the core of Source.

- I watched Source create the universe and everything in it. The entire universe—all of what we consider to be physical matter—exists solely within Source's mind and imagination. Everything, including the human species, is manifested through the power of Source's almighty abilities.

- Each one of us is one of Source's own subpersonalities utilized during incarnation to weave Source's self-awareness into manifested physical matter creatures and things. We call ourselves "souls" when we are incarnated. We are not manifestations; we are part of the ultimate reality of Source as an entity. We are not now, and never have been, separated from our Creator.

- I believe I was given a mission in the afterlife to return to Earth to tell anyone who will listen what I learned there, including about manifesting and how it differs from prayer and law of attraction theory.

- Other near-death experiencers were also given small bits of Knowings about manifesting, but not as extensive as what I brought back from the afterlife.

3

What Is Manifesting?

MANIFESTING IS THE MENTAL PHENOMENON BY which Source creates and maintains what humans, and other universe inhabitants, perceive to be physical matter. I learned in the afterlife that everything in the universe is manifested. The sun, moon, and stars are manifested through Source's thought Energy. The Earth, and everything on it, is manifested by Source's thoughts. The human bodies we inhabit are manifested by Source via thought Energy. Nothing in the universe actually exists as solid matter independent of its manifestor. Nothing in the universe even exists outside Source's mind. Everything we behold—both collective human reality and individual human realities—consists solely of Source's thoughts and imagination.

We souls are parts of the same mind that manifests physical reality. Therefore, we can manifest physical matter too. We are Creators!

The Nature of Thinking

Most of the biomechanics of human life are automatic, consisting of chemical reactions orchestrated by DNA. Most human behaviors are prompted by physical drives, which are also chemical reactions within the body. Humans have the ability to think with their organic brains through the process of transfer of electrochemical energy over nerve cells. Human thinking is thus the product of chemical reactions. It consists primarily of matters important to species survival—eating, drinking, sleeping, sheltering, recreating, and procreating. Human intelligence consists of cunning, strategy, and manipulation, the same as every other animal on earth. Many humans are also highly trainable through education to use and expand upon bodies of knowledge accumulated by the combined human/soul minds.

We Light Being souls inside humans are aware of our bodies' thoughts because we can hear them enunciated in our combined body/soul minds in the same voice we hear coming out of our hosts' mouths. This mental monologue keeps up a constant chatter, commenting on what the body sees and hears and judging people and things; replaying a song stuck in memory; puzzling over how to solve a problem or make a decision; remembering past events; and survival planning. Some of these thoughts are the body's. Some are ours.

Everything else you have ever thought to be an aspect of human intelligence and thinking does not belong to humans at all. True intelligence belongs solely to Source. When we Light Beings incarnate into physical matter, including into humans, we invest the body with a small part of Source's mind and intelligence. The part of Source's mind we identify as our own Light Being personality/character pours into the flesh while in the womb. Our own/Source's mind then fuses with the organic mind and body of the human animal we inhabit to create a seamless thinking machine. A Light Being soul mind is not limited to the brain or even the nervous system. Our mind diffuses throughout the physical body, thinking and storing memory everywhere within the body as well as everywhere within our Light Being multiple levels of awareness. Our Source thinking is responsible for mathematics, science, linguistics, music, art, dreaming, intuition, eureka! moments, and creativity of every type. The only human-body contribution is to express Source's intelligence and creativity through its physical abilities.

Although these bodies cannot co-opt our Light Being thinking powers, we souls often get essentially the same result by default because the amnesia we suffer during incarnation prevents us from realizing we are not the bodies we inhabit. We souls think we are human even though our levels of awareness still in the afterlife know better. Because of amnesia, we believe the human thoughts marching across our combined body/soul minds belong to us. We believe we are limited to the data we obtain through physical senses with which to construct our thoughts. In short, our thinking is strongly influenced by human thinking and limitations, with the end result being that we use our superior intelligence and creativity in our pursuit of animalistic lives. That does not mean, however, that our host bodies have access to our spiritual powers, including the ability to manifest physical reality. They do not.

Manifesting Is a Spiritual Power

The ability to manifest physical matter and physical reality is a power unique to Source. It is divine. Manifesting occurs when Source, or one of its subpart Light Beings, tunes its "attention and intention" to creating physical matter. Chapter 5 explains how to consciously use this spiritual power. We souls primarily use it unconsciously, as discussed in chapter 6.

The power to manifest is an innate ability we Light Beings share with Source because we are literally parts of Source—we are extensions of its self-awareness. Source manifests the physical world. We do too as Source's role-playing mental characters. Manifesting is an awesome spiritual power that resides in the part of us Light Beings incarnated as human souls, as well as in the parts of our Energy/consciousness/levels of awareness that remain in heaven during incarnation.

I learned that there is a group of Light Being characters within Source who have a particular interest in Earth and its inhabitants, whom I call "All Those With An Interest In Earth." Every Light Being serving as a human soul is included in this group. In other words, we Light Being parts of Source collectively co-create the physical world we know as Earth. All Those With An Interest In Earth collectively manifest the default physical matter that humans and other earthen creatures perceive as this planet. Humans believe the world will be the same when they wake up as it was when they went to bed. They also believe that all humans see and perceive the same physical scenery. Humans believe that conversations, and pictures and videos, confirm that there is an objective reality out there that is the same for everyone. Therefore, All Those With An Interest In Earth maintain via their thoughts and imagination essentially the same physical environments from day-to-day because that is what the manifested earth creatures believe in and accept. The variations in physical presentation over time are attributable to the operation of Source-designed processes, including gravity, weather, and biology.

We Light Being souls manifest physical reality and physical matter during the time we temporarily occupy human bodies. We use manifesting to craft our own version of reality as well as to contribute to the collective co-creation of the physical matter Earth we all experience. If we are not manifesting consciously, we are doing so unconsciously, accepting the default settings of the physical world as Source and All Those With An Interest In Earth create it.

We have all witnessed our own manifesting while we sleep in what we call dreams. We are "out of our minds" during sleep. Out of our human minds, that is. Knowings informed me that dreams fulfill a number of functions, one of which is to allow us souls to continue to explore human life while our host bodies repair and recharge through sleep. Some of the little movies we call dreams are actually out-of-body living in temporarily manifested environments. Most of the time these environments mimic familiar scenes from waking life, or perhaps scenes from books we have read or videos we have seen.

I learned in the afterlife that after crossing over into the Light some souls may continue to manifest physical-like environments and experiences while they remain in what I call "human mode." A soul newly arrived in heaven must go through a transition process: (a) to reacclimate to its true nature as one part of a Light Being's multiple simultaneous levels of awareness, and (b) reintegrate the soul Energy with the rest of the Light Being Energy and awareness that remained in heaven during the soul part's incarnation. Until that process is complete, the soul most likely will believe it is still a human being and be limited to thinking the same way it did in human life. In other words, the soul will stay in human mode. Consequently, souls often manifest earth-like surroundings in the early stages of their afterlife transition. That is why some near-death experiencers report seeing physical settings like on Earth while visiting the afterlife. They have manifested the scenes and experiences they expected to see, in the same way they were used to doing it while ensconced in human bodies. Differences in our expectations of life after death, and our beliefs about what we personally deserve in the afterlife, account for the variations in physical scenery some manifest there. Once we accept that we can continue to live without physical surroundings, we stop manifesting them.

Humans Try to Get What They Want

Humans cannot manifest physical reality. Not with their brains. Not with the subconscious. Not through *human* willpower, work, emotions, thoughts, or anything else. This is because humans themselves are manifestations. They exist because Source imagines them and maintains them in its mind. Human animals are not parts of Source's consciousness and self-awareness. Humans have no afterlife. Only we Light Being souls inhabiting humans return to a state of awareness that humans call heaven or paradise.

Humans have no power to create physical matter. Nor are their bodies even capable of understanding manifesting. We souls have to set aside the human way of thinking and adopt Source's perspective in order to understand how its manifesting power works. You will never understand manifesting, or be able to consciously use it, if you cannot rotate your beliefs 180 degrees from thinking you are the human body you occupy to knowing that you are a part of Source awareness occupying that body. Whenever you ask yourself, "How do I link to my soul or inner Source in order to manifest?" you signal your inability to accept who you really are. If you think you possess a soul, you display your resistance to accepting the truth about your identity as Source. When you try to communicate with someone out there in the universe who is separate from you, like a God, you are stuck in human mode. You still believe you are the body you see in the mirror and you will not master conscious manifesting with that belief.

Human animals have needs and wants that go unfulfilled every day. Wouldn't it be nice if humans had a way to get everything they want, every time they want something? As Light Being souls inside humans, we retain a dim recollection that this is possible. But we cannot remember manifesting or how to do it. So, using our combined body/soul minds, we have over the ages of incarnating into humans crafted creative schemes for getting what we think we want, with varying degrees of success. Here are some familiar methods:

Wishing. The first tool we use in childhood to meet our unfulfilled needs is wishing: *"Star light, star bright, the first star I see tonight, I wish I may, I wish I might, have the wish I wish tonight."* We wish that our parents, grandparents, Santa Claus, the Easter Bunny, God, or whoever will give us what we want. Wishing is a normal part of human life. Our parents probably taught us to wish and encouraged it. Wishing out loud can serve a useful purpose, such as informing our parents and others of our needs and wants.

Prayer. Prayer is the religious model of wish fulfillment. Prayer proposes that we ask a God who is separate from us to grant our wishes. This is a traditional belief founded upon the mistaken assumption that we are separate beings from God and dependent upon a human-like male divine being to control our lives. There is absolutely nothing wrong with holding this belief. It is normal during human life. Most of us Light Being souls think this way because we assume everything in spiritual life is just like what we see in human life. Holding this belief is a very human thing to do and, after all, we incarnate into humans in order to experience life as they do.

But in the afterlife I learned a completely different truth about our relationship to Source/God. One that gives us much more hope and power. I learned that there is no humanoid "God" *out there,* apart from us. Our Creator, Source, is not a separate being from us and never has been. So when we couch our supplications in the form of pleas to an Almighty who "art in heaven," we preserve the age-old myth that God is separate and apart from us. That type of prayer not only denies the truth of Source's existence but our powerful role within Source. *We* are Source. *We* are the God to whom we pray. In effect, we are praying to ourselves, asking ourselves to grant our own or our hosts' wishes.[14]

Perhaps we are actually praying to the core entity Source—the massive Energy field with far greater power than our own small sparks. Although this concept makes more spiritual sense, it casts some parts of Source into the role of being separate from the rest of Source, as well as having separate powers. It would be more accurate to say that we are praying to the part of ourselves remaining in heaven and to "all of us as Source," because this construct at least does away with the idea of separation. And, it gets us back to the truth that we ourselves have the power to manifest reality.

Variations on the prayer approach suggest that our attitude in making the prayer could affect its outcome. Presumably, fervent supplication, or praying with gratitude or humble belief in God, will affect Source's judgment whether or not to answer the prayer. In other words, the religious model is the human model. It assumes that Source thinks and acts like humans do and is influenced by the same types of emotional manipulation that affect humans. Nothing could be further from the truth.

The Law of Attraction. The law of attraction is a theory of wish fulfillment more similar to prayer than manifesting. This theory claims we attract things and events into our lives via the content of our thoughts. The law of attraction presupposes that there is a law of nature that magnetizes human thoughts and that God or the universe responds to that magnetic pull by producing the human thinker's object of desire. Law of attraction theory is a step above the religious model in that it attempts to give us more control over the outcome of our prayers by using a clearly misapplied scientific principle. But it too is based entirely on human perspective—humans believe they see a separation looking up toward Source/God from down here. According to the law of attraction, you still follow the religious model of fervently asking for objects of desire. The recipient of your prayers may be the universe instead of God. But that does not disguise that, at its core, the law of attraction is a modified religious model. The allure of this theory is that God's discretion is supposedly taken away—this mythical law supposedly *forces* God/Source to give us what we want.

The problem with these human tools is they often bring us to a false conclusion or leave something of major importance out of the picture. Human-based beliefs are by definition limited to human perspective. I was shown in the afterlife that humans are in the absolute worst position to know what is good for them because they operate primarily in the present moment. They rarely think ahead to consequences and often do not apply what they have learned through past experience.

All the human ways of magically getting what we want rely upon someone "out there" to give it to us. What if there was a way we could get what we want all by ourselves? Well, there is. It is called manifesting. The explanation I provide gives you the broader perspective—the spiritual perspective—that is necessary to actually consciously participate in the physical matter manifesting process.

Manifesting Furthers Spiritual Goals

The primary use of manifesting in human life is to create opportunities to experience the aspects of humans we Light Beings seek to know more about, or to complete the mission or task we have chosen for ourselves. In other words, we use this spiritual power to fulfill our purpose for being here.

Before I died, I thought that everything in life means something, every event was designed to teach us something, every person was presented to us as a potential teacher, and our task was to ferret out what it is we are supposed to learn in each instance. I was astounded to learn in heaven that most of the events of my life as Nanci had no meaning whatsoever. They were just human animal experiences. I was told that we incarnate into humans simply to see what their animal lives feel like, not because they have anything to teach us. While incarnated, we Light Beings will automatically manifest the opportunities we need to satisfy our spiritual goals. But those events may be few and far between. Most of our human lives will not be goal related, especially if we are here for a limited purpose. In other words, our goal-directed manifesting does not take up much of our lives or prevent us from pursuing non-goal-oriented manifesting.

When I entered the afterlife, I did not find myself in the phase of eternal life from which we Light Beings incarnate, as other NDErs have. I did receive Knowings about incarnation, however, and I remembered at least one of my own incarnation decision events as those Knowings downloaded. I learned from these Knowings that we Light Beings generally select one of the three following spiritual goals for each human lifetime, depending upon how many times we have incarnated into humans before.[15] If we are fairly new to incarnating into human animals, we select a unique aspect of life or a specific human trait to be our chosen "theme" to study and then choose a series of successive hosts whose lives will provide different vantage points on that theme. Those Light Beings with more human incarnation experience may agree with one or more Light Being friends to incarnate with them to provide loving support as the friend faces the challenges of a particular physical life. We thus take a supporting role in the drama of their human life. If we have had extensive incarnation experience, we may agree with one or more Light Being friends to incarnate with them to perform a specific task at some point in our Light Being friend's human lifetime. We essentially take a walk-on role in their drama.

The most complicated and time-consuming goal is studying a certain aspect of human life, a chosen theme. In order to do that, we souls inside humans have to repeatedly manifest into our hosts' lives various opportunities to study that theme. We do it in cooperation with other Light Being souls. But we souls often fail to recognize our own manifestations, and consequently, fail to take the opportunities presented. If so, we just try again.

Perhaps a Light Being wants to study how it feels to experience extreme contrasts in self-esteem and chooses human parents who give birth to a beautiful girl named Sally living in a small town. Sally makes friends easily in school, is homecoming queen in high school, joins a sorority in the local college and is chosen to ride as a princess atop a parade float, and marries the man of her dreams. All the events of her life have pumped up her human sense of self-esteem. Now she has to lose it all in order to meet the goal of feeling extreme contrast. Sally and her husband may at the spiritual level co-manifest the opportunity for him to transfer to a big city as part of a huge promotion at work that he cannot turn down. Our princess moves to an environment where no one knows her, lots of women are beautiful, her husband works sixty hours a week, and she cannot find a job. Her self-esteem takes a dive and the spiritual goal is met.

Alternatively, perhaps the soul inside Sally agrees at the spiritual level with another Light Being that the two of them will co-manifest an auto accident that severely disfigures Sally. She lives in constant pain, refuses to go out, her friends drop away one by one as she avoids them, and her husband leaves her for a woman who still has her looks. The manifested accident could also show the former princess the extreme opposite of high self-esteem.

As another option, the soul inside Sally may manifest opportunities for her body to become obese and her face bloated. No one wants to put her front and center on a parade float anymore. Her husband starts avoiding her. Her friends are polite but talk about her behind her back, saying, "What happened to Sally?" Over time, Sally loses all her self esteem, just as she, the soul, planned.

The soul in our example may manifest opportunities for all three of these alternatives to occur but her host body may be running the show, as is so often the case. Her body may decide not to leave her small town and chooses to lose her husband rather than her comfy nest of ego boosters. Or her body decides at the last minute to drive another way on the day of the to-be-manifested accident and avoids the collision altogether. Or, her body may ignore all the opportunities to become fat and start taking extreme exercise classes instead. That is why it takes repeated manifested opportunities for any of us souls to achieve the experiences we seek to study. You may have noticed that you get yourself into the same types of situations over and over in your life. You find that problems repeat themselves in different settings. Or you run up against the same difficult personality type wherever you go. Many spiritual authors will tell you this is because you are supposed to learn something from these repeated experiences. Actually, it may just be that these experiences tie into the theme you are collecting data on and this is exactly how you get different perspectives on that theme.

A soul taking a supporting role in another Light Being's incarnation may agree to incarnate with that other Light Being for the purpose of being that other soul's human mother, father, lover, marriage partner, therapist, or spiritual advisor, or to take some other role in which the soul can provide the support that the two agreed in the afterlife would be provided. In this situation, the supportive soul may be only a co-manifestor with the supported soul and have no other purpose in human life.

Fulfilling the third type of incarnation goal may require only a few minutes or hours of human life to accomplish. For example, two Light Beings may agree to incarnate together with one pursuing a theme requiring multiple incarnations and the other agreeing to perform an important task that furthers the other's theme. An example might be a soul that comes into human life to perform a lifesaving surgery so that a Light Being friend can experience what it is like to survive a deadly accident. The two souls, together with the rest of their Light Being Energy still in the afterlife, will manifest the accident so the surgery can be performed. The rest of the friend soul's human life has no purpose at all other than to simply feel what human life is like.

There is no real purpose to human life other than to meet our own spiritual goal, whether it be studying a theme of human life, being a support person to another Light Being we love, or being a catalyst for a short while in another soul's human journey. Otherwise, all of us Light Beings incarnate because we enjoy the challenge of trying to be true to our innate spiritual nature in the face of overwhelming emotional and physical animal drives. We want to see how well we handle various problems and decision points. We want to observe ourselves managing conflicting emotions—ours and our bodies'. We are curious about our ability to inject unconditional love into human relations. And we want Source to feel its manifestation through us.

Sometimes our purpose for incarnating can be accomplished in its fullness only through having experiences that are painful to both us and our human hosts. You cannot use human logic to understand why we Light Beings would choose to experience pain because it was not the human who made that choice. It was an entity with wildly different character traits and logic. Just like you cannot use bumble bee logic to understand why dogs chase cars, or cat logic to understand why whales beach themselves, you cannot use human logic to understand why Source finds events and emotions that horrify humans to be interesting.

To my surprise, I received Knowings in the afterlife that there is no karma. No destiny. No predestination. No path we should follow. No right or wrong choices that will get us into heaven or not. We parts of Source have absolute free will to create our incarnated life as we see fit. We also have the free will to allow our host body to live its animal life without our conscious input. We are Source and have almighty freedom of choice.

Manifesting Does Not Fulfill Human Greed

We use manifesting to serve our spiritual purposes, not human greed. It is not a get-rich-quick scheme, as some might hope.

Manifesting is not a magic trick. Magic exploits the weaknesses in human senses to create the illusion that something has appeared out of thin air. The rabbit pulled from a hat existed prior to the magic trick and was concealed in a hidden compartment. Manifesting, on the other hand, actually does create physical matter out of thin air—from Source's thought Energy. And manifesting creates the air as well!

Manifesting does not involve pretending. Manifesting creates everything that humans experience as believable. It is the only reality humans will ever know.

Manifesting is responsible for what humans call the range of experience from good luck to a miracle. It is also responsible for everything from bad luck to tragedy. Manifesting creates all of our physical matter experiences.

Manifesting is not wish fulfillment or the simple creation of a desired object or sensation. We Light Being parts of Source have the spiritual power to manifest sudden wealth, a new car, or a mansion to replace our current human possessions, and leave everything else about our life intact. But that is not how Source and we parts of Source use the power. We use manifesting to further our goals and purposes for incarnating. If material possessions do not further those objectives, we do not manifest them into our lives.

In sum, Source uses manifesting to create the universe and everything in it. We Light Beings participate in Source's creation of physical matter and human reality. And because the universe consists entirely of Source's thought Energy, changing our Light Being thoughts within Source's mind changes the physical manifestation. Therefore, we souls can change our hosts' manifested lives.

Manifesting can be used consciously and unconsciously to improve our human lives in ways great and small. We can bring more comfort and happiness to this living adventure. We can change just about anything we do not like about our lives, so long as our fellow Light Being co-creators who are involved with or affected by the change agree with us to do so. Like any spiritual endeavor, conscious manifesting requires concentration. Manifesting while we are encased in our human hosts also requires preparation. The types of preparation we need are addressed in chapters 5 and 6. But first, we must disabuse ourselves of a belief that we *attract* people and things into our lives.

Important Takeaways from Chapter 3

- Manifesting is the mental phenomenon by which Source uses imagination and creative intention to create and maintain in its mind what humans and other universe inhabitants perceive as the physical universe.
- Only Source can manifest physical matter. We Light Beings can do it only because we *are* Source.
- Humans are manifestations.
- Manifested human animals have their own thoughts. We Light Being souls inside humans have our own thoughts. Only Light Being thoughts can be manifested into physical reality, not human thoughts.
- Manifesting is a spiritual power that cannot be used by humans to get rich. We souls use manifesting to achieve our spiritual goals and reasons for incarnating into humans. We can also use it to increase our comfort and happiness.

4

Law of Attraction Theories

WHILE I WAS LEARNING ABOUT MANIFESTING IN the afterlife, it became clear to me that Source had given this information to incarnated souls before, but the message had been distorted by human interpretation and wishful thinking. At the time I had no idea how or why manifesting was so misunderstood. I had never heard of it before. It was not until twelve years later, while I watched the much-touted video promoting the book *The Secret,* written by Australian TV producer Rhonda Byrne, that the cylinders clicked into place.[16] I then understood how human thinking had converted a spiritual power of the Light Being soul into a get-rich-quick scheme. That video showed me that various authors and speakers have been spreading the word about something they call the law of attraction. The current iteration of it presupposes that Mother Nature magnetizes human thoughts, makes them vibrate at different frequencies based on subject matter, and allows their magnetic pull or vibration to draw out of the universe the pre-existing physical matter that matches the human thought vibration. I immediately recognized this thinking as a human misperception and misstatement of the spiritual act of manifesting physical reality.

When I was inside the core of Source's mind during my 1994 NDE, I relived Source's memories of imagining the universe. I witnessed Source impressing upon manifested physical matter various laws of conduct to govern its behavior. I thus have firsthand knowledge that Source did not create a law of attraction. There is no law of attraction in operation in the universe. Humans do *not* attract what they want from an invisible eBay in the sky. Thoughts are not magnets. We are not on the receiving end of any type of wish fulfillment dynamic. Instead, we Light Being souls *create* our own individual realities and physical matter lives through the spiritual power of manifesting. The tremendous difference between the law of attraction and manifesting lies in who holds the power. *We* hold the power over our lives, no one else does.

Background on Law of Attraction Concepts

Before I died, I believed that we attracted life's events to us, especially the negative ones, as though we are bad luck magnets. I wholeheartedly believed that something I was doing unconsciously attracted hurtful people into my life and I was powerless to stop it. I thought it had something to do with my energy, either physical or spiritual. But I learned by dying that none of this is true and that these ideas came from a human theory that there exists a law of nature called the law of attraction. By later reading the most popular authors offering this theory, I learned that it evolved over generations from a couple of later disproven pseudo-scientific theories that were popular more than one hundred years ago.

The Theory That Thoughts Become Things

One of the oldest authorities on the law of attraction is *The Master Key System*.[17] In 1912, Charles Haanel, a successful businessman and author with no science education, used the then well-known term "the law of attraction" to denote what he believed to be one of many immutable laws of nature—the idea that thought will manifest into form. This concept continues on in law of attraction lore. At one point in *The Secret*, published in 2006, Rhonda Byrne says that thoughts *become* things. This claim is nearly true, but not for the reason Ms. Byrne proposes. *Source's creative thoughts* become things through the spiritual power of manifesting physical reality. Human thoughts do not.

In my opinion, Haanel was one of Source's messengers about the spiritual power of manifesting. However, he is also a perfect example of how we Light Being souls can lose our way and embellish kernels of Universal Knowledge with human logic. Because amnesia prevents us from knowing the full eternal truth, we assume what we observe and experience within humans must be true about the afterlife as well and weave it into our spiritual belief systems. That is what Charles Haanel did. He filled in the gaps in his understanding of manifesting with his own conjecture about human physiology and the relationship between body and soul. For example, Haanel erroneously theorized that humans relate to the soul through the human subconscious mind, which he thought was located in the solar plexus. This, like most of Haanel's theories of human anatomy and physiology, has been scientifically disproven since 1912. The more important point here is that Haanel understandably but erroneously bases his law of attraction theory on the belief that we who manifest are human and therefore separate beings from our Creator.

But Haanel correctly recounts the eternal truth about manifesting when he writes: "There is but one consciousness in the universe able to think; ... As this consciousness is omnipresent, it must be present within every individual; ... your consciousness is identical with the Universal Consciousness, or, in other words, all mind is one mind."[18] Haanel reasoned that because there is only one consciousness, and when it thinks it manifests physical matter, then "the ability of the individual to think is his ability to act on the Universal and bring it into manifestation."[19] Here we have the origin of the idea that human thoughts manifest and become things.

Haanel describes manifesting, although he calls it the law of attraction, in his 24-week correspondence course later published as *The Master Key System*, as follows:

> The law is that Thought is an active vital form of

> dynamic energy which has the power to correlate with its object and bring it out of the invisible substance from which all things are created into the visible or objective world. This is the law by which, and through which all things come into manifestation.[20]

Haanel again refers to manifesting when he says: "Things are created in the mental or spiritual world before they appear in the outward act or event. By the simple process of governing our thought forces today, we help create the events which will come into our lives in the future, perhaps even tomorrow."[21] Haanel understood that Source's thoughts manifest physical reality, and that Source is the only consciousness. But he needed a way to explain how humans, whom he believed to be separate from Source, could get their hands on that manifesting power.

Like other writers of his time, Haanel guessed that the right kind of thought works to *attract* the "substance" God/Source/Universal Mind uses to create physical reality. He likens this substance to the attractive forces that hold atoms and molecules together. That substance, of course, is Source's thoughts. Haanel theorized that the human subconscious mind (soul) creates reality by attracting "substance" from the Universal Mind. Using the concept of attraction made perfect sense to a man who did not know that Source resides inside the human animal in the form of a Light Being soul. How else were humans to obtain this mysterious substance to create matter if not by attracting it? Haanel lacked the Knowings that we souls are not separate from the Universal Mind and therefore have no need to bridge any gap between it and us through attraction. Haanel's explanation of the law of attraction, therefore, mistakenly hinges on our alleged need to attract the magical substance that we souls use to manifest reality. Because we are literally Source itself, we already have control over Haanel's substance that creates physical matter—Source's creative thoughts. But Haanel's theory that human thoughts attract the substance that creates matter became one of the springboards for modern day law of attraction theory.

The Get-Rich-Quick Scheme

The Master Key System refutes the current idea that the law of attraction is a get-rich-quick-scheme that brings us material goods, like money and cars. Haanel acknowledges that wealth is a product of labor, and that the more we put into our work and the more we work to promote the best for other people, the more wealth we will get in return. Haanel explains why we have seen that the law of attraction does not work every time. He repeatedly debunks the notion that we can use manifesting for selfish human purposes. He equates the law of attraction with the law of love. He states: "The trained mind knows that every transaction must benefit every person who is in any way connected with the transaction, and any attempt to profit by the weakness, ignorance or necessity of another will inevitably operate to his disadvantage."[22] He adds: "Success is contingent upon the highest moral ideal, which is 'The greatest good to the greatest number.'"[23] And: "Whatever you desire for yourself, affirm it for others, and it will help you both."[24] In other words, Haanel's law of attraction follows Light Being character traits, not human greed.

Manifesting generally creates circumstances and opportunities in our lives, not material goods, as a 3D printer does. Haanel states: "The law of attraction will certainly and unerringly bring to you the conditions, environment, and experience in life, corresponding with your habitual, characteristic, predominant mental attitude."[25] In other words, manifesting creates our human lives in accordance with our deeply held thoughts and beliefs. In addition, Haanel repeatedly emphasizes that thoughts must reflect the Truth (what I call Universal Knowledge) in order for them to manifest.

How did Source's divine message about using manifesting to create physical reality come to be *The Secret*'s "easy paths, tips, and shortcuts" to building wealth?[26] Through human misinterpretation and wishful thinking.

In the 1930s, Napoleon Hill, then a young magazine journalist with no science background, was commissioned by Andrew Carnegie to interview five hundred rich and successful people in order to document the effectiveness of Carnegie's own secret formula for succeeding in business and amassing wealth. Hill generally refers to the Carnegie success formula as "the secret," the name later adopted for a book on the law of attraction by Rhonda Byrne. The unifying theme Hill noted in his interviews is that the wealthy men all pursued their dreams of success with a dedication and drive that consumed them. Hill's job was to develop a formula others could follow to financial success. To do so, Hill borrowed freely from Haanel's *The Master Key System.* Combining Haanel's spiritual and pseudo-scientific theories with information gleaned from his interviews, Hill created a thirteen-step wealth-building program detailed in his 1937 book *Think and Grow Rich!*[27]

Napoleon Hill did not actually write about the law of attraction, though his book *Think and Grow Rich!* formed the basis for Ester and Jerry Hicks's Abraham books. Hill's book is about using human talents and good business strategy to work within the manifested world to generate personal wealth. Hill explains that wealth (unless it is inherited) depends upon a person coming up with a great moneymaking idea and following through with definite business plans to bring that idea to fruition.

Haanel's and Hill's ideas have made their way into the most famous of the law of attraction theories, those of Ester and Jerry Hicks and of Rhonda Byrne. Byrne's book, *The Secret*, is full of testimonials of believers who say they used the law of attraction to create their own success stories and wealth. And many other authors have followed suit. Upon reading these books, I understood why Source thought it so important that it correct erroneous statements about manifesting. I further understood that later law of attraction proponents unfortunately built on Haanel's erroneous scientific theories rather than on his accurate statements about manifesting. This is how Haanel's message that we create our own physical reality transmuted over time into a wealth building tool.

The Theory That Thoughts Vibrate

Various spiritual authors, and even I in my own books, have used two words that readers have taken literally, and concretely, because that is how humans think.

The first word is *vibration*. When most of us read or hear the word vibration we automatically think of cell phones, vibrators, foot massagers, tuning forks, piano strings, or those vibrating beds that older motels used to have. We envision something physical that quickly moves back and forth, or jiggles.

The second word is *frequency*. When most of us read or hear that word, we begin to think of radio waves, microwaves, or sound waves, which have frequencies that can be tuned up or down a scale.

Combining the two words into the term "vibration frequency" and applying it to thoughts can create the false impression that thoughts are similar to radio waves and can be tuned, or to sound oscillations that can be raised or lowered. The thoughts of Light Beings, souls, and humans cannot be tuned or raised to a higher frequency or oscillation. No one can increase or decrease the amount of Energy in one of Source's thoughts.

Unfortunately, law of attraction believers have adopted Napoleon Hill's theory that thoughts have a vibrational signal as a way to explain how humans attract Haanel's "substance" that creates matter. Many such authors have not dispelled their readers' misperception that they use the words vibration and frequency in the scientific sense. Some of these authors may not even realize that they misunderstand the terms themselves, having fallen into the trap of human concrete thinking. Some honestly believe the scientific phenomena of vibration and frequency do apply to non-physical constructs such as thinking. These authors are read by other authors, who then perpetuate the idea, creating a whole body of work based on an error in semantics.

Charles Haanel used the term vibration in *The Master Key System* in the sense of attunement or alignment, not a physical oscillation back and forth. Haanel believed that correct thoughts could essentially bring one into alignment with the flow of Energy from the Universal Mind and complete something like an electrical circuit that allows abundance to flow through. Thus he claims that vibration is the action of thought, not necessarily a physical property of thought. His *Master Key System* is based on the belief that we are separate from our Creator, and therefore need some kind of conduit between it and us. Haanel was never made aware of the Knowing I received in the afterlife that we are never separate from Source. No electrical circuit or aligment is needed.

Napoleon Hill's speculation that thoughts vibrate differently according to their subject matter has been adopted as fact by law of attraction authors and proponents. But Hill's present-day followers admonish us not to take the vibration concept literally, that is, in the scientific sense, because it will lead us to false conclusions about thoughts. The Editor who reconstructed the original 1937 version of *Think and Grow Rich!* for republication, commented that when Hill mentions vibrations of thought, he means the electrochemical impulses in the brain, not vibrations like radio waves. The Editor writes: "'Vibration of thought' is how Hill chose to describe the complex, little understood process by which electrochemical impulses in the brain create and convey 'thoughts' and 'emotion.'... It would be a mistake to attempt to understand such terms as 'vibration of thought' in a strictly literal sense."[28]

Ester and Jerry Hicks attribute their law of attraction philosophy (their word)[29] to information Ester believes she channels from a group of spiritual beings she collectively calls "Abraham." But Jerry Hicks explains in *The Astonishing Power of Emotions* that his spiritual author career sprang from his financial motivational speaker business based on Napoleon Hill's *Think and Grow Rich!*. Jerry Hicks taught Hill's principles for twenty years before he went into the spiritual author business with his wife.[30] Hicks acknowledged that most of his seminar participants did not get rich, so he looked for the missing element that secured Carnegie's success. Logically, the missing element from most people's success stories is a great moneymaking idea. But Jerry Hicks did not focus in on that. He acquired an older edition of *Think and Grow Rich!* and compared it to his well-read copy. Hicks discovered that edits to the original edition had repeatedly deleted the word "vibration."[31] He therefore assumed that the concept of "vibration," rather than having a great moneymaking idea, was the key to making Hill's wealth building plan work. It is not surprising then that the Hickses say Abraham channeled to Ester Hicks that every thought vibrates, radiates a signal, and attracts a matching signal back because of the law of attraction.

The idea of vibrating thoughts is a human myth. It is not scientific fact. Nor is it spiritual fact, according to everything I learned in the afterlife. And the law of attraction theory based on this vibration idea is invalid.

While privy to Source's memories of Creation, I learned and felt the nature of Source's thought Energy. It is nothing like radio waves, sound, or any type of physical matter that vibrates in the sense that humans use the word. Source's thoughts have no physical mass. Rather, they are mental Energy and felt like Energy to me. I used the terms "vibrational level" and "Energy signature" in my books to have a shorthand way to refer to the different slices, levels, layers, or points in the infinite continuum of Source's Energy field that I felt. Those Energy points closer to Source's core seemed to me to feel lighter, to be more excited, and to have more life, comparing them to my human experiences with physical world energy. Those Energy levels farther away from the core felt denser and less excited. I conceptualized this phenomenon as waves of Energy radiating from a core, like the sun's rays, with the strength or density of Energy dissipating the farther away from Source's core it is. I never meant for the word *vibration* to be taken literally or understood in the same way that we understand physical matter vibrations. There is simply no accurate word in human language to describe Source Energy because it is not a concept within human experience. The best I can do is to describe how it felt to me by using imperfect words and hope that my readers get the gist of what I am saying.

I was given Knowings during the Creation review that everything in the universe has something like an Energy signature (a term I borrowed from *StarTrek*), which is merely a label to identify its manifested nature, form, and—for lack of more accurate words—speed and density. When I say something that Source is thinking, such as the universe, has vibrational levels or Energy signatures, I do not mean these terms in the sense they are customarily used. Thoughts do not vibrate like vocal cords or tuning forks vibrate. They do not have measurable energy like electricity or wind. And they do not have frequencies like radio waves. The very idea of an Energy signature, or vibration, conveys a human observation about certain types of physical matter that does not accurately apply to Source Energy or thought. But these words are the closest analogy in human language that I have found to discuss something so far outside the human experience. I use "vibration" as a nickname, not a statement of scientific fact.

From Source's perspective, the universe is pure thought and has no vibration. But manifested creatures in the universe have physical senses that perceive other manifested things and creatures differently depending upon their form and density. Humans see some forms of Source's manifested thoughts as more solid or denser than others. A wooden table is more solid than water. Dirt is denser than air. One could say that tables, water, dirt, and air all have different and distinctive Energy signatures or vibrational levels—so long as it is understood that those differences are judged only by how human sensory organs perceive them. Yet all of them are pure Source thoughts and nothing else. Creatures with different sensory organs may well perceive tables, water, dirt, and air very differently than do humans. But the manifested forms that tables, water, dirt, and air take remain the same regardless of who or what perceives them because of their Source-given identifying Energy signature/vibrational level.

From a human's perspective, physical matter creatures and things have identifiable Energy signatures or vibrational levels that allow humans to recognize them by form. For example, rocks have one Energy signature and human animals have another. That is how humans tell rocks from people and recognize various persons, places, and things. All things or creatures in the same category share the same Energy signature or vibrational level. In other words, all human animals have the same Energy signature or level of vibration that corresponds to the human form. There is no importance, no order of priority, and no hierarchy among different Energy signatures. Trying to assign one is human competitiveness. An inanimate object or creature cannot, for example, move up or down vibrational levels because its Energy signature is its fixed identity within the manifested world. Nor can a human increase his or her vibrational level or Energy signature. If it were even possible, the core entity Source would have to do it. And the result would be a human's transformation into some type of non-human physical matter, not a more valuable human vibration or a spiritual level closer to Source.

I learned in the afterlife that thoughts, whether human, Source's, or Light Being souls', do not vibrate in the physical sense, much less vibrate at different frequencies depending upon subject matter content. Source's manifestations in the physical universe have identifying characteristics that I call Energy signatures or vibrational levels. But Source's thoughts that manifest these creatures and things do not actually vibrate.

Spiritual law of attraction proponents claim that vibrations on the same frequency attract each other. "Like attracts like," they declare. As a pilot who once relied on radio signals for my safety, I know that for a radio signal to transfer from point A to point B, one point has to have a transmitter and the other a receiver. Many electronic devices (like phones) are transceivers, performing both functions. Any radio operator will tell you that when two simple radio signal sources try to broadcast on the same frequency, they interfere with each other, not attract each other. Once again, saying that thoughts on the same frequency as a desired object will attract it is a false scientific spin.

Individual human thoughts do not vibrate even though they are associated with electrochemical reactions in the brain. Functional MRIs can identify the areas of a brain that are involved when a patient responds to certain visual or emotional stimuli, but to my knowledge no scientific instrument has ever measured an individual thought's vibration. Human thoughts have no vibrational frequencies, much less different frequencies depending upon the content or subject matter of the thought. Believing that thought vibration is possible has led many authors to construct a law of attraction that does not exist.

The Idea That Thoughts Are Magnetic

Another one of *The Master Key System's* erroneous scientific explanations appears to be the genesis of subsequent law of attraction theory that thoughts are magnetic. Charles Haanel writes: "The predominant thought or the mental attitude is the magnet, and the law is that 'like attracts like,' consequently the mental attitude will invariably attract such conditions as correspond to its nature."[32] Magnetism is Haanel's guess for how humans attract physical matter "substance" from Source via the vibrational electrical circuit that Haanel thought existed.

Napoleon Hill believed Haanel's erroneous spiritual theory that thoughts vibrate at different unique frequencies, and added that when mixed with enough emotion, thoughts create a "magnetic" force. Hill writes: "Thoughts which are mixed with any of the feelings of emotions constitute a 'magnetic' force which attracts other similar, or related thoughts."[33] Hill spoke of attracting more thoughts—not objects of desire. But Hill went a step further and concluded that humans can attract thoughts from each other's minds, what he calls the "thought vibrations of existence," to add to and bolster a specific thought until it dominates the mind. He writes:

> From this great "storehouse" of experience, the human mind is constantly attracting vibrations which harmonize with that which DOMINATES the mind. Any thought, idea, plan, or purpose which one holds in one's mind attracts from the "thought vibrations of existence" a host of its relatives, adds those relatives to its own force, and grows until it becomes the dominating, MOTIVATING MASTER of the individual in whose mind it has been housed.[34]

Hill's thought-snatching theory is based on an unwarranted expansion of the results of an experiment in telepathy. Duke University conducted research in 1934 into the existence of clairvoyance, which is the soul's ability to see with the mind. The Duke experiment consisted of a tester sitting in one room thinking about one of five cards with a shape on it, and a test subject sitting in another room trying to "see" the shape on the tester's card using mental telepathy. The experiment had nothing to do with reading another person's creative thoughts. Nevertheless, Hill extrapolated from this limited science to a generalization that humans can pull any kind of thought right out of each other's minds.

If Hill's idea about stealing thoughts were true, nothing could be kept secret in our world! Inventors would have their inventions stolen by anyone who thinks about the subject matter of the invention with a strong desire to gain the inventor's knowledge. Songwriters and playwrights would have their intellectual property in progress stolen by anyone who attracts thoughts about songs or screenplays with greed. Corporate espionage could be conducted by a businessman leaning back in his chair, his feet on the desk, thinking about competitors' products while feeling wronged and vengeful. And there would be no need for investigations of any type because police and detectives could simply brainstorm with anger about how a crime was committed and the perpetrator's thoughts about how the crime was achieved would be attracted to them. Worse, if we are feeling blue and walk by someone who is suicidal, we may begin thinking of killing ourselves. Or, if we are grieving and go to a support group, we might be consumed by all the grieving thoughts of others in the room.

I believe Haanel and Hill use the term "magnetic" to describe thoughts by analogy, not as a scientific fact. These authors gave voice to the everyday observation that humans can think in linear fashion, connecting related thoughts in what we often call a train of thought. I think this is what they meant about thoughts being magnetic. Thought A quickly gives rise to related thought B, which pulls in tangentially related thought C, etc. A chain of thoughts is formed centering on a common theme. Hill would say the train of thought then dominates the mind enough to become a motivating or driving force. This type of thinking requires concentration on a specific topic, not magnetism.

Your own life experience has taught you that more often than not thoughts do not attract other thoughts on the same subject unless you are making a conscious effort to solve a particular problem, or are obsessively ruminating about something that upsets you. Take a moment to pay attention to the thought monologue running through your combined body/soul minds. You will see that your thoughts jump all over the place with no apparent subject matter connection. Trains of thought run from one tangentially related thought to another. We make leaps of logic. We speculate. Our minds switch from one topic to another with lightning speed. Our minds wander. They do not pick a topic and attract other thoughts on the same topic unless we specifically concentrate on doing just that.

Later authors, including Ester and Jerry Hicks, expanded upon Hill's speculation that thoughts vibrate, are magnetic, and when mixed with strong emotion can pull thoughts out of someone else's mind. They theorized that human thoughts could pull physical matter manifestations out of Source's mind or the universe. Once again, the Hickses credit Abraham with the following message: "*The Law of Attraction* and its magnetic power reaches out into the Universe and attracts other thoughts that are vibrationally like it ... and brings that to you ... All of these things are brought into your experience through a sort of powerful magnetic funnel as they are vibrational matches to your own thoughts."[35]

The Secret's law of attraction philosophy is based on similar ideas of previous authors, including those of Charles Haanel (1866-1949), author of *The Master Key System*, and Robert Collier (1885-1950), author of *The Secret of the Ages*. *The Secret* also claims that thoughts not only attract other thoughts on the same subject, but also attract actual physical matter objects like cars and cash. Byrne believes that thoughts are magnetic, have a frequency, and magically attract all *like* physical matter things throughout the universe that are on the same frequency. Byrne therefore uses the same false scientific magnet and radio frequency theories as her predecessors.

Law of attraction proponents claim if we align our thoughts with our human desires, then the desired object will be drawn to us like a magnet draws iron filings. No scientific data backs up this claim. No clinical research has ever proven that a magnetic force draws life's experiences to us. This is a pseudo-scientific belief that was held in the late 1800s by writers who had no scientific training or proof of their theories at the time they wrote. For example, Prentice Mulford (1834-1891), author of *The White Cross Library*, a former gold miner, cook, and school teacher is credited with the idea that thoughts running in currents can attract similar currents of thought. He also referred to thoughts as unseen magnets that could attract their corresponding match in physical matter. *The Secret* is based in part on this book. That thoughts are magnetic is a philosophical concept outdated by time and advances in science. Yet it persists in the law of attraction arena.

Science has shown that magnets attract either their polar opposites or things that are not themselves magnetic but which by physical nature are drawn to a magnetic field, such as iron filings. For thoughts to act like magnets, everything we want to draw to us would have to likewise be magnetic and have the opposite polarity, or be compositionally drawn by a magnetic field. Magnets of the same polarity repel each other. So, if thoughts truly were magnets, they would normally attract their polar opposites. We would attract the exact opposite of what we want. Alternatively, thoughts would attract only those things that by nature are drawn to a magnetic field—like iron filings. A simple test can prove that money, for example, is not attracted to a magnet or magnetic field. Take an ordinary magnet and try to pick up dollar bills, checks, stock certificates, certificates of deposit, credit cards, gift cards, or any other evidence of wealth. The magnet does not pick up paper or plastic money. Now try it with coins. U.S. coins are not attracted to magnets either. If an actual magnet cannot attract money, how could magnetic thoughts do it?

Though it is true that scientists have identified and measured an extremely weak magnetic field emanating from the brain, the explanation given is that it is caused by the flow of ion currents from neuron to neuron inside the brain.[36] The magnetic field is not generated by thoughts, but rather by the chemical reactions of ions moving within the physical brain. These chemical reactions have nothing to do with the content of thoughts. To the extent that one believes thoughts can occur only in the brain, it might make sense to theorize that these ion flows moving chemicals make "thoughts" very weakly magnetic. But the magnetic pull ranges from one hundred millionth to one billionth the strength of the Earth's magnetic field—a far cry from the strength needed to attract a car or bag of money from somewhere in the universe, or even steal other people's thoughts.[37] For those of us who have been out-of-body, and were still able to think, the science of magnetic thoughts falls apart. So does the theory that thinking occurs in the brain. NDErs and out-of-body experiencers prove that we Light Being souls can still think while outside of our host bodies.

While I was inside Source's mind reliving its memories of Creation of our universe, I saw that Source did not directly create stars, planets, creatures, or things. Instead, Source projected its thought Energy and then impressed upon it what we would call laws of nature to govern manifestation of the universe. The application and operation of those laws of nature resulted in the physical universe we now see. While I witnessed the physical evolution of the universe, I observed certain types of matter attracting other types of matter due to gravitational force. I saw that electro-chemical bonds were created among atoms and molecules, holding them together. I witnessed the magnetic attraction that some types of matter had for other types of matter. These are all processes that Source created to govern physical matter. But I personally witnessed that Source did not create any type of attractive force or bond between human thoughts and other thoughts within the same mind, or between one human's thoughts and thoughts in someone else's mind, or between thoughts and items of physical matter within the manifested universe. Source did not create a law of attraction for the universe. The idea that thoughts attract things is a human attempt to explain the observed results of the spiritual phenomenon of manifesting.

Magnetism is a property of certain types of physical matter. Thoughts have no physical matter. They have no weight. No mass. No size, shape, or form. They have no chemical composition and therefore no way to have magnetic bonds between protons and electrons. Thoughts are an aspect of *consciousness*, not physical matter.

The Concept That Emotions Attract Matter

Napoleon Hill believed the energy of the universe has the power to transmute human thoughts into their physical matter equivalents. But he also knew that his interviewees were highly driven to succeed. So he theorized that only thoughts that have been made strong enough to dominate the mind lead to wealth, and then, only if supported by strong faith and belief. Hill observed that strong emotions and belief in a great moneymaking idea helped make it dominate the mind enough to be a driving force.

Hill hypothesized from his interviews with wealthy men that strong human emotions are necessary to amass wealth. He writes: "It is not only those thought impulses which have been mixed with FAITH, but those which have been mixed with any of the positive emotions, or any of the negative emotions, that can reach and influence the subconscious mind."[38] Hill wrote that faith, love, and sexual desire are the most powerful emotions to use to bolster one's belief that he/she will indeed receive his/her desire by following the great idea and business plan designed to bring it to fruition. Hill was under the illusion that the blending of these three emotions speeds the order (like from a catalog) of what one desires to the subconscious (where presumably the soul resides), where it is changed into a spiritual equivalent that God will respond to by transmuting the thought into physical matter. Hill believed that frequent repetition of one's thoughts would develop faith in their achievement—regardless of whether those thoughts are constructive or destructive.

Ester and Jerry Hicks were so convinced of Hill's theories, which Jerry Hicks taught for twenty years, that they incorporated his belief about emotions into their own version of the law of attraction. Hill wrote: "All achievement, no matter what may be its nature or its purpose, must begin with an intense, BURNING DESIRE for something definite."[39] The Hickses call this concept their "definite desire" principle in the Abraham material and have crystallized it into one of their laws of nature.

Some spiritual authors claim that thoughts also create our feelings. From there, they launch into an explanation that we can control our feelings by simply controlling our thoughts. For example, *The Secret* claims that when we feel bad, the law of attraction must bring more bad things into our lives. The author reasons that because emotions are caused by thoughts, and thoughts attract like thoughts from the universe, then the universe is sending more emotions to us to let us know whether we are tuned to a good or bad frequency. In effect, *The Secret* says all we have to do to be happy is *be happy*—as though we could produce that emotional state at will.

I learned in heaven that it is not true that our emotions arise from human thoughts. Shortly after I arrived in the afterlife, a huge quantity of Knowings about human nature and my own spiritual nature downloaded into my mind. I received Knowings that human emotions arise in response to external or internal stimuli, not thoughts. They are automatic and nearly instant. Source built hair-trigger emotions into the animal survival instinct as a protective feature for creatures subject to wild and varied threats to their lives and well-being, such as those humans encounter on Earth. We Light Being souls have separate, and more complex, emotions. Knowings made very clear to me that emotions are innate in both human and spiritual natures. One by one I compared my old familiar human emotions with those I felt in heaven. All were present and accounted for with the exception of fear and the emotions and drives inherent in the survival instinct, such as greed, envy, and lust. Fear and greed were identified to me as fonts of related emotions unique to manifestations with a survival instinct. In other words, any thought or feeling that smacks of fear or greed is human in origin. Any thought or feeling that conveys unconditional love or acceptance is Light Being in origin. While we are inside these physical bodies, however, we Light Being souls experience both sets of emotions, our own and our bodies', sometimes at the same time. We may call contradictory emotions "having an angel on one shoulder and the devil on the other," because we feel torn in two directions. I have never read anything about the law of attraction that recognizes there are two sets of emotions at work. No spiritual author I have read even seems to be aware that we souls have emotions separate from human ones. Consequently, these authors attribute all emotion to the animal and believe human emotions to be as powerful in spiritual life as in animal life. They are not.

The Abraham-Hicks teachings and *The Secret* also claim that feelings are communications of how the universe has judged our thoughts. The authors believe the manifested inanimate physical matter universe can communicate with us, and, that it has the tendency to render judgments that humans would make. Emotions can tell us a lot about our own feelings. But the analysis of them comes from us, not from somewhere or something out there in the universe.

Some spiritual writers state that our emotions tell us whether we have hindered or facilitated our connection to Source. According to the Hickses in the Abraham series of books:

> You can *feel* whether you are allowing your full connection to Source Energy or not. In other words, the better you feel, the more you are allowing your connection; the worse you feel, the less you are allowing your connection. Feeling good equals allowing the connection; feeling bad equals not allowing the connection—feeling bad equals resisting the connection to your Source.[40]

The Hickses use the term "connection" in this context to mean being aligned with Source's vibration. Source is defined as an "eternally expanding vibrational Stream of Well-Being from which all that is, flows."[41] Source is correctly identified by these authors as the Source, or Creator, of everything in the universe. But their connection theory is anchored in the human belief that we Light Being souls are separate from Source. We souls do not have to facilitate our natural connection to Source, whether by thinking good thoughts or feeling good or otherwise, because *we are Source*. We have never been separated. We have no bridge to gap. We are connected, one to the other, because we are all one entity. Similarly, humans are Source's own thoughts. There cannot be any greater connection to Source.

Law of attraction proponents are embroiled in human thinking when they attribute to human emotions the spiritual power to summon physical matter. Knowings informed me that manifesting has no emotional component at all. It is an entirely intellectual, mental, spiritual ability. So it does not matter what our human emotions are about a subject. Nor does it matter what our spiritual emotions are about it. Whatever our emotions are, we need to get them out of our way in order to concentrate on exercising our manifesting power.

The Idea That Spiritual Beings Provided These Theories

Many believe the law of attraction is an eternal truth revealed to mankind by spiritual beings in the afterlife. That is not the case.

When I first started reading *Ask and It Is Given: Learning to Manifest Your Desires*, by Ester and Jerry Hicks, I thought the book was going to be about manifesting physical reality. To me, it reads like a few kernels of Universal Knowledge sprinkled into a bushel of human theories based on comments made in *Think and Grow Rich!*. The collective Abraham books' law of attraction theory is essentially prayer, fortified with references to alleged laws of the universe that make it sound as though Source is compelled to answer our prayers. We all know from experience that this does not happen that often.

The Abraham-Hicks philosophy also draws concepts from other spiritual authors well known in certain circles in the late 1980s. For example, for several decades earlier a woman named Dorothy Jane Roberts believed she channeled a spiritual being named Seth. The *Seth* material added an entirely new dimension to law of attraction theory. Seth claimed that we create our own reality based upon our beliefs. This is true, as I learned in the afterlife. But Jane Roberts's

Seth character, like Haanel and Hill, also proposed that thoughts are electromagnetic and can be used to draw wealth to us, which is not true.[42] The Hickses were enamored with the Seth books. Shortly after reading them, Ester and Jerry Hicks met with Sheila Gillette, who similarly believes she channels information from a group of twelve archangels she calls "Theo." Theo told the Hickses that they too could channel their own guides by meditating, which is how the Abraham spiritual origins idea took form.[43] Ester and Jerry Hicks combined the Carnegie/Hill wealth building material with the idea of channeling information from spiritual beings to create their own brand of law of attraction philosophy.

I have been fortunate enough to have had far more and deeper spiritual experiences than any of the law of attraction writers I have read, including those mentioned here. My several visits to the afterlife and multiple out-of-body experiences allow me to put into a much larger context what law of attraction proponents have understandably, though mistakenly, represented to be spiritual truth. I believe Source intends that I explain to others why the law of attraction theory falls short of spiritual truth about manifesting. The basis for my belief is that while I was in the afterlife I was allowed to experience Knowings about manifesting three times, in three different ever more deepening ways. And, right before I spiraled through an Energy hurricane back into my body, I had been thinking, "Somebody ought to tell those people [back on earth]." And here I am.

I received massive amounts of data during my 1994 NDE. Knowings downloaded into my mind as complete, intimate knowledge of whichever subject I consciously or unconsciously chose. Everything about a given subject was revealed to me, not just answers to discrete questions. The information was nonverbal and felt as though I had gained the knowledge through personal experience, not telepathy. I have returned to the afterlife several times since 1994 and received Knowings in the same direct way. A few times, I have also received small bits of information from Universal Knowledge while in this body, although this latter sensation was nothing like getting Knowings in the afterlife. Still, in my experience, tidbits of Universal

Knowledge do *not* come through communication with any type of spiritual being, such as Seth or Abraham. Knowings informed me that no human can channel thoughts of Light Beings living in the afterlife. We Light Being souls can, however, download small amounts of information at a time directly from Universal Knowledge. That information does not come through a spokesman, or spokes-spirit. If we souls access Universal Knowledge while in a human body, the information will appear in our minds without words.

After reading many of their books, I believe channelers have at times downloaded small bits of spiritual truth from Universal Knowledge just as all souls can do. But most of the time, I believe, they hear their own thoughts as the Light Being soul inside the body and misidentify them as coming from souls in the afterlife. Here is how I came to this conclusion: in one of their books, the Hickses describe meeting Sheila Gillette and explain how she channels by laying down, relaxing, and releasing her consciousness so that the non-physical Theo can speak through her.[44] In other words, Ms. Gillette relaxes and enters a meditative state. Ester Hicks describes her own initial channeling episodes in a similar way. These ladies who claim to be channelers enter a meditative state, which I know makes it easier for them to hear their own Light Being soul voices. For Ester Hicks, it was the first time in her life that she experienced the effects of meditation. She knew nothing of Source's self-awareness residing as souls inside manifested human animals. She had never directly experienced the duality of body and soul. She had never before heard herself thinking as a soul. All she knew was that the thoughts she believed she channeled were different than the run-of-the-mill human thoughts she was used to having. So she reasonably assumed her own spiritual thoughts were those of an outside being—someone in the spirit world.

My guess is that during meditation the soul inhabiting Ester Hicks's body combined the Knowings it has from Universal Knowledge with knowledge of Napoleon Hill's book, plus the works of other channelers Ester has studied, into a philosophy that Ester mistakenly believes was given to her by spirits in the afterlife. Unlike humans, we Light Being souls have total recall of everything we have ever experienced, including all communications and sensory impressions. And we souls can use any of that information even though the body cannot consciously recall it. In my opinion, it would be very natural for a channeler to assume that information available to her as a soul because of its total recall could have come from some outside being, especially a spiritual being. Nearly everyone who has had an out-of-body experience, or spiritual experience through deep meditation, assumes they have entered a spiritual world or realm in the process. Instead, these souls simply escaped the drudgery of human thinking and stayed in the manifested physical universe. That mental freedom does make it easier for us souls to access Universal Knowledge. It does not, however, put us in contact with anyone in the afterlife. Nor does it give us the ability to perfectly understand the information we obtain. In other words, these types of experiences merely give us awareness of our own thoughts as the soul inhabiting the body. Most soul thoughts are generally based entirely on human experience, not great insights from Source or the spiritual world.

Please do not misunderstand me here. I know these spiritual authors have unselfishly devoted their careers to trying to help other people become successful. I respect and honor them for that. I do not mean to denigrate them or imply they are deliberately telling their readers untruths. My belief is that they have honestly done their very best to give the world something they believe will help everyone improve human life. We all should be so generous. However, based on everything I learned in the afterlife, the far broader and deeper context of spiritual understanding I was given, my literal merger with Source, and my own out-of-body and meditation experiences, I believe that channelers are mistaken about the source of their information. Our thoughts as souls are frequently different than the human routine daily monologue. And, while a few of our own thoughts may be accurate statements of Universal Knowledge, the souls of channelers, like all of us, have been so indoctrinated with human-based beliefs that they have adopted human speculation as spiritual fact, when it is not. Channelers, like all of us, have been affected by amnesia as to the truth of Source and physical life. Thus they have no way of knowing that their own thoughts as Light Being souls have human origins. Of course, the only reason I have this wider perspective on the subject is because I have been gifted with multiple afterlife experiences that answered all my spiritual questions. I have done nothing to earn or develop the information I was given. It was simply poured into my mind. My only contribution to the effort was working hard to remember as much of it as I could while I was being stuffed back into Nanci's cold, dead body.

I also know that any Light Being close enough to the incarnation phase of eternal life to communicate with the part of its Energy inside a human has a somewhat limited understanding of Universal Knowledge—limited enough that I would not trust it. I was astounded to learn that my own understanding of the Knowings I received in heaven changed dramatically the longer I was there. I mentally went through a transformation from understanding like a human would to understanding like a Light Being, and then, finally, Knowing as Source. It never occurred to me before I died that souls or spirits in the afterlife would not be all-knowing and understand all of Universal Knowledge perfectly. I was shocked to learn that those souls residing in the phase of afterlife from which we incarnate do not even know their own nature and identity as characters within Source's mind. They still believe they are separate beings and identities from Source. It was not until I lived through afterlife stages beyond the one from which we incarnate, and then returned my Energy to Source's core, that I first awakened to the truth that I was never a separate being. That I was never outside of Source's mind and imagination. And that I am Source itself pretending to be the character I know as my eternal personality. Thus I do not fault anyone for drawing spiritual conclusions that contradict Source's own truths if they arrived at them before reaching the awakening stage I experienced. It simply is not possible to understand Universal Knowledge perfectly until this awakening. I believe this is why Source designated the part of itself that I claim as my own eternal personality to explain the thinking errors inherent in religion and the law of attraction. I may be the only soul that has experienced this awakening process and returned to a human body with the memory of it.

We have now traced the origins of present day law of attraction theory and have shown that it was constructed brick-by-brick from previous authors' philosophical and spiritual beliefs. It was not communicated from the afterlife through human channelers.

Manifesting vs. Law of Attraction

Most of the questions I receive about manifesting arise because people confuse manifesting with the law of attraction. This is a natural consequence of concepts contained in *The Secret* and the Ester and Jerry Hicks books making their way into mainstream spirituality.

The following statements show some of the basic distinctions between manifesting and the various law of attraction theories:

Manifesting is a spiritual power we Light Being souls inside human bodies have because we are Source's consciousness. As extensions of Source, we collectively create from Source's thoughts all that we experience as the physical world, all the interactions we have with others, and all the significant events in our lives. The law of attraction philosophy is a human theory featuring inaccurate statements about the properties of magnets and energy frequencies in combination with spiritual beliefs—none of which I found supported by Knowings I received in the afterlife.

Law of attraction proponents claim that whatever thought your human mind holds is creative at the spiritual level and mandates that the content of the thought be attracted into the physical world because it is already created in the spiritual world. Human thoughts, however, do not create physical matter. All physical matter creation comes from Source, some via its Light Being parts. Nor do human thoughts govern what we Light Being souls manifest into physical reality. We souls manifest only what we truly and deeply believe about ourselves and life.

There are no magic human words, mindsets, or emotions involved in creating our lives. We have to get the human mind, emotions, and body out of the way in order to manifest.

The law of attraction claims humans can attract what they want from the universe, when, in truth, human animals cannot manifest anything. Humans are manifestations. Manifesting has nothing to do with aligning vibrations. There are no cars, better jobs, a Mr. or Miss "Right," or bags of money floating around in outer space that we can attract by tuning our physical, mental, or emotional vibration to the right frequency. The universe is a manifestation. It has no power to send us the objects we desire.

Manifesting will not make us rich. Following the law of attraction will not either, otherwise we would all be rich! But conscious manifesting does make our lives richer in the types of experiences we want to have.

Important Takeaways from Chapter 4

- The law of attraction is a very old human-designed theory or philosophy of life. It did not originate with Source or any of its Light Being mental characters, whether incarnated or in the afterlife.

- Physical matter properties like vibration, frequency, and magnetism do not apply to thoughts because thoughts are an aspect of awareness and not physicality. We Light Being souls are still able to think when we are outside physical bodies.

- Thoughts are not magnetic because they have no physical matter that could be magnetic. They have no mass, no weight, no size, no shape, no form, and no chemical composition. They do not attract anything, much less items of desire from somewhere else in the universe.

- Thoughts do not create emotions. Both humans and Light Being souls may have emotional reactions, and strong ones, in response to thoughts. But I learned in the afterlife that Source imbued both manifested human animals and Light Beings with emotions that respond to external and internal triggers, including thoughts.

- Human emotions, such as strong desire, have no impact on our spiritual abilities as Light Being souls to manifest reality. Manifesting is an intellectual, mental, spiritual ability completely separate and apart from any human or Light Being emotions we may experience.

5

Consciously Manifest Physical Reality

TO LEARN HOW TO CONSCIOUSLY MANIFEST OUR lives while inside humans, we Light Being souls need to shift our awareness from the daily chatter running through the combined body/soul minds to our own thoughts alone. We must elevate our mental perspective to the spiritual state—that is, rise above the human level of awareness—to engage our manifesting power. When we are in our natural spiritual state of mind, we have a very different understanding about life than we do while inside human bodies perceiving the world and life from their limited viewpoints.

Manifesting can be conscious or unconscious. Consciously taking control of your manifesting comes in two forms: (a) you can presently focus your attention and intention on manifesting a specific event or opportunity for yourself as discussed in this chapter; and/or (b) you can consciously work to change the beliefs you hold about life, and the part you play in it, so that your unconscious manifestations will follow healthier beliefs. Either way, what you as Light Being soul truly and deeply believe about yourself and life controls what you manifest. This chapter explains the spiritual principles of conscious manifesting and provides a formula for manifesting a specific experience or opportunity. The next chapter explains how to create a happier life by actively changing hindering beliefs to healthier beliefs from which to unconsciously manifest.

Manifesting requires only these two spiritual acts: attention and intention. Attention and intention do not have to occur at the same time. Nor does the attention part of the formula always require only mental effort. You can use human body forms of paying attention, as mentioned below.

Attention

Like the rest of Source's mind, we mental characters manifest reality by focusing our attention and intention on what we as Source want to experience. *Attention* can take any form that mentally engages us in the topic of interest, including focusing our thoughts, visualizing what we want to create, researching the subject, and talking about the subject. An example would be to research a disease to manifest healing from that disease. The research will give you known treatments and parameters of improvement so that your manifestation will take a form that is believable to you. You will be directing your attention to what works so that you can boost the known treatment's healing properties using manifesting Energy. If you are an action-oriented person who focuses best through movement, taking physical action to further what you want to experience can be your form of mental attention. For example, if you want a job, you should look for one. Read want ads, send out résumés, go on interviews, etc. This will not only focus your attention, but also position you to recognize your manifestation when it appears in the marketplace. You might see the perfect job opening posted online or at your current place of employment—but only if you look for it. You may want to use several forms of attention together until you find one or more that works best for you.

A one-word summary of the attention half of the manifesting formula is "focus."

Tune out everything around you, the same way you tune out squabbling kids while you are working on something. The same way you tune out the TV when you have it on just for background noise. Tune out the world like you tune out annoying noises. Simply deafen yourself to its existence.

Concentrate the same way you do when threading a needle, or programming a computer, or studying for a test. Put all of your awareness on what you want to manifest using continuous concentration.

Relax your mind the same way you do when watching a beautiful sunset or gazing over the limitless waves of the ocean while on vacation.

You can strengthen your mental focus muscles. If you played music while doing your school homework, that was a focus-strengthening exercise. Some video games require focused attention and train the mind to exclude everything outside of the game. Performing surgery, mountain climbing, flying an airplane, defusing a bomb, and deep-sea diving all develop focus because of the risk of loss of life associated with inattention. Repeatedly doing anything that requires constant attention to the task is a focus-strengthening exercise. Driving should be done with focused attention but usually is not, so it does not count. Weight lifting, mowing the grass, cleaning, and other tasks that you know you can do without paying much attention to them may allow you to meditate but they do not help strengthen your focusing skills. Learning to meditate will give you the best tools for dedicating mental and spiritual attention to manifesting. *The Master Key System* includes a series of mental exercises or meditations to help Haanel's students obtain the mental clarity and control needed to consciously manifest reality. I recommend these exercises to you if you have trouble clearing your human mind during meditation. You can obtain a free PDF version of the original edition of *The Master Key System* correspondence course from the website www.masterkeysystem.com.

Manifesting requires Light Being soul mental attention, not the attention of the human mind, emotions, or physical senses.

Intention

The word *intention* has several synonyms relevant to manifesting: goal, aim, design, end, motive, objective, plan, point, purpose and will. In short, you mean to make it happen. You will it to happen.

My experience, both while in the afterlife and in this body, is that the more important half of the manifesting formula is intention. By this I mean you, as a character/personality within Source's mind, exercising your will to create in physical matter and reality the object of your attention and focus.

Your intention must be spiritually creative intention—the type of intention that only Source can have—to create physical reality. Creative intention is not desire, hope, wishing, or any other form of wanting something to happen *to* us. Manifesting is a spiritual mental power we Light Being souls possess. It is not affected by, and does not respond to, human desire or emotions. Without spiritual, creative intention, we Light Beings do not manifest physical reality.

The highest form of creative intention is expectation—certainty at our level of existence within Source that a thing will exist or an event will transpire. Why? Because expectation expresses deep belief and manifesting always follows beliefs. In the afterlife you can expect a beautiful garden and instantly be in a beautiful garden. This is why NDErs who have crossed over and gone into the Light may report that they roamed through an exquisite garden, heard otherworldly music, were bathed in exotic colors, or encountered religious figures. Those expectations were in their minds as they were going through the Light. Because these souls were in spiritual form at the time, they were able to instantly manifest their beliefs into physical reality in heaven. I did the same thing shortly after I entered the Light. The only difference is that I realized while I was doing it that the physical environment appeared in response to my conscious thought about it. NDErs universally affirm that the physical environments they experience in the afterlife feel just as real as those they experience on Earth. I know mine felt just as real. These reports confirm the Knowings I received in the afterlife that the physical world is a manifestation.

Mental Effort Is Required to Manifest

Some law of attraction authors make it sound like manifesting physical reality requires no more than a thought or dream about what you want, or maybe creating a collage of pictures that depict your desires. This attempt to make manifesting sound easier has misled many and prevented them from even beginning to consciously manifest a better reality for their lives.

Manifesting requires concentration, focus, and dedicated will—all words that describe mental effort. Manifesting is effortless when we are outside these bodies. But inside them we must do the slight amount of work it takes to pay attention. Haanel's *The Master Key System* admonishes us: "Concentration is much misunderstood; there seems to be an idea of effort or activity associated with it, when just the contrary is necessary. … You should be so interested in your thought, so engrossed in your subject, as to be conscious of nothing else."[45] This mental effort is no harder than thinking through and solving a problem, or cramming for a test, or planning a party. You have done it a million times in other contexts. Now apply that same concentration to improving your life.

If this degree of dedication to a goal is required for manifesting, how can it be true that we are always manifesting? The answer is that we form the creative intention at our Light Being level of awareness—the part of us that stays in the Light while another part of us is invested into a human as its soul. Each of us intended to have certain experiences before part of us incarnated into the human we now occupy. That purpose becomes a driving force in the human life we create. We are also capable of creative intention at the soul level of awareness. We souls unconsciously manifest our beliefs all of the time. Our present manifested life results from the efforts of both the part of us still in the Light and the part of us inside the human. It is this latter part, the part of us influenced by human beliefs, that manifests the results we can learn to control.

Manifesting Principles

Manifesting follows truly and deeply held beliefs, not thoughts. We Light Beings manifest into physical matter what we truly and deeply believe about ourselves and the world we live in.

We do it from memory. We do it by habit. We rarely look at this data much less change it. We simply manifest what we are used to experiencing in human life. It is like the movie *Groundhog Day*: each morning we manifest whatever we believed about life before we went to bed. Consequently, day after day we replicate the same manifestations we unconsciously created at some forgotten time in our human host's past. This is why some illnesses and injuries remain long after they should have healed. And it is why so little changes for most people, no matter how much they try to attract what they want.

It does not matter what your day-to-day thoughts are—unless, of course, they reflect your truly and deeply held beliefs. And it does not matter what mental chatter runs through your mind. Nor does it matter how you word your thoughts, positively or negatively, or if you repeat affirmations and positive-feeling statements. It does not matter that you obsess about certain topics, curse in your mental chatter, or hold nasty thoughts about others. How you feel about your thoughts is just as irrelevant as the thoughts themselves. The only "thoughts" that matter, the only ones that contribute to manifesting physical reality, are the beliefs you hold at the moment.

We do not manifest random thoughts. We do not have to worry about every little thought that rolls across our minds. We do not manifest random thoughts. And we do not manifest any human thoughts. We unconsciously manifest our beliefs. And we consciously manifest only what we give our attention and creative intention to manifesting.

Those authors who admonish that every thought and feeling we have attracts more of the same to us are thinking like superstitious humans, not conveying wisdom from the afterlife. In *The Secret*, Rhonda Byrne claims: "If you think unkind thoughts about someone else, *you* will experience those unkind thoughts manifested."[46] This is erroneous. We manifest our Light Being soul beliefs, conscious and unconscious, rather than the thoughts of our combined body/soul minds. While in heaven, I was quite astonished to learn that few of our thoughts while inside humans are important in the grand scheme of things.

Manifesting satisfies spiritual goals, not human desires. Various books proclaim that we can draw material goods into our lives via a theory called the law of attraction. I learned in the afterlife that there is no spiritual power that allows humans, or even Light Being souls inside humans, to get rich quick or manifest human desires.

Manifesting follows Light Being soul desires, not human ones. We use it to further our incarnation goals. There exists not a single Light Being soul on earth that really needs or wants a luxury car, a big house, a bracelet, or a pile of money. Source is not interested in material wealth. A reader once asked me whether it is possible while inside a human to manifest vast wealth if our intention is to fulfill spiritual goals. Since it is very rare even to be aware of our spiritual goals, we cannot know whether material wealth will further them. Material goods are not necessary, or even relevant, to most of our spiritual goals. So if a Light Being does manifest these types of riches into an incarnated life, it is because they are part of the lifestyle necessary to gain the experiences chosen for this incarnation, not because a human body desires them.

If you chose a lifestyle of being in a monastery, you could diligently apply the law of attraction principles until the cows come home and still not manifest a jet, a 125-foot yacht, winning the lottery, or any other form of material wealth because doing so would be inconsistent with your chosen subject of study. The theme or genre of experiences for a human lifetime is chosen by the Light Being serving as soul, not the body. Law of attraction books do not tell you this because they are not based on the spiritual principle of manifesting. They do not tell you that you will only manifest those things that further your spiritual goals, or that fit with the specific task you chose before incarnation, and are logical for the lifestyle of the human being whose life you have decided to share. Is it possible for a monk to manifest a jet plane? Absolutely. But for a monk to retain ownership of a jet in his life as a monk? Not very likely. It would be pointless for a soul inside a human monk to manifest this type of luxury, and, therefore, it would serve no spiritual goal.

We manifest only our own reality, no one else's. We cannot manifest bad things into someone else's life. We cannot manifest good things for someone else. So our monk in the last example would not manifest the jet plane for his monastery to sell. We manifest only our own lives, our own experiences. Human nature causes us to want to control other people's lives. We want to "make it better" for our children. We want to stop other people from hurting us. We desire better living conditions, more appreciation for our efforts at work and home, and the best life has to offer for our loved ones. Yet we cannot manifest any of those things into the lives of our children, colleagues, or loved ones. Only they can do it.

Similarly, other people cannot manifest anything into our lives for us. One reader asked me whether a person could acquire a positive character trait, such as leadership or wealth, if the people around him regarded him as a leader or wealthy. No, someone else's belief that we have positive qualities or wealth will not manifest them for us.

We can, however, manifest *jointly* with one or more other Light Beings (see chapter 9) by making agreements at the spiritual level moment-to-moment while we are living human life. My afterlife lessons did not teach me a way to consciously enter into these spiritual agreements while inside a human, or even how to influence their formation or outcome at the spiritual level. Still, I attempt to do so by asking Light Beings who love me to add their attention and intentions to mine to manifest a specific result.

Everything that happens is the result of a free will choice we souls have made: we consciously chose it, we unconsciously chose it, we agreed at the spiritual level to experience it, or we chose to do nothing but allow a human animal life play out without our conscious input.

We manifest opportunities more often than we manifest things. I learned in the afterlife that while we are in human bodies we are far more likely to use our power to manifest opportunities for experiences rather than things. Clearly, we have the ability to co-create mountains and rivers and forests galore with All Those With an Interest in Earth. But our personal manifesting endeavors generally revolve around creating the circumstances or events that will logically produce an experience that meets our spiritual goals. We then have to make the most of the opportunities we manifest. In order to do that, we have to be aware of those manifested opportunities. We have to "tune in" to our lives. Expand our awareness. Pay attention to that little urge that we should do something, or go somewhere, or say something right at that moment.

For example, you may be lamenting that your vacation plans fell through and now you have time off from work but nowhere to go. For reasons you cannot fathom, you repeatedly feel an urge to go to the grocery store. You do not really need anything from the store. You do not feel like going. You tell yourself that it is just not worth it to get dressed and truck off to the store when you cannot even think of anything to buy. So you stay home. Had you gone to the store, however, you would have run into a friend whose vacation plans also fell through, and who is stuck with a lakeside cabin he cannot use because he has to work. Although you did not manifest a physical matter vacation spot, you did manifest the opportunity for someone to offer you the use of one. Ignoring that urge to go to the store prevented you from becoming aware of the results of your manifesting.[47]

To create something entirely new in your life, like a new job or new home, you use the same tools. Use attention to figure out what the new thing might be like. Try a lot of different ideas to get clarity about what you want to create. This may take some time if your idea is pretty vague, such as: "I want a new job where people appreciate me and I can advance in pay and responsibilities." You have to get a handle on what kind of job your body can do and what is available in your area of interest. Talk to your friends about what they do for a living, watch the news, and talk to placement services about the types of jobs with openings. Consider signing up with a temporary placement agency to get a feel for what types of jobs exist in your locale and what they are like. Take placement exams to find out what your skills and interests are so you can match them up with the available jobs. All this effort is not required to manifest a new job, but it may be required to know where to find your manifestation and/or whether it is really what you want. Research what types of goods and services are likely to be needed in the future. You will have to do the legwork to find out where the current version of the future might be headed. Now that you are set to figure out what the current situation is, you can begin to mentally create what you want, whether it currently exists or not. It is possible to manifest a new job that has never existed before, but if that is what you want, be prepared to put in time until the world catches up with you. Even Facebook was not an overnight success.

Some spiritual, and not-so-spiritual, authors urge us to have "money consciousness" in order to get ourselves into sync with the great generator of wealth, whether you believe that to be the physical universe or God. But, in the words of *The Master Key System*: "Wealth is a product of labor. Capital is an effect, not a cause; a servant, not a master; a means, not an end."[48] These statements are more in line with how we Light Beings think. When we choose to enter into a human life, we know human society runs on various forms of money or goods to trade. Thus we recognize that having money is a necessary element of human life. But we attach no significance to amassing wealth because, as the saying goes, "You can't take it with you." Most of us Light Beings have no interest in manifesting wealth into a human animal's life. The spiritual authors mentioned above are thinking like humans, not conveying any spiritual guidance, when they tell us how to attract money.

Many questions that readers ask me about manifesting relate more to making choices between potential manifestations than the manifesting power itself. A reader might have to make a selection between this job and that one, this house and that one, this relationship and another one, taking this action or that action. The soul manifested the opportunity for a reason. The reason might be because one of the two choices fits with its goals for this human life. Or the reason might be that the soul is challenging itself to turn down two choices that are not right for it. Make selections of this nature based on what resonates with you or feels right spiritually at the time. But whichever choice you make, it will not be wrong. If your spiritual intention was to accept choice A, and your body chose B, you will simply manifest another opportunity in a different context at a later date and get another chance to choose.

Personal example: When I was about to graduate from law school I had two job offers with large, prestigious law firms in different cities. I wanted both jobs. I could not decide between them because my emotions kept getting in the way. One city was my hometown, where all my high school and college friends lived. The other was where I went to law school, worked part time as a law clerk, and lived with my mother and brothers. To resolve the dilemma, I pretended for one week that I had already made the decision to stay in City A and planned accordingly. I rented an apartment, got my car out of hock with the mechanic, and signed up for the bar exam study course. The next week I pretended I had made the decision to return to my hometown City B. I drove there and rented an apartment, picked out my office furniture at the law firm, and signed up for the bar exam in that state. At the end of each week I sat very still and just let my feelings about the week wash over me. When something is right for me, meaning it is congruent with what I intended to experience this life, I get one of two reactions to it during meditation: (1) I get very excited about it and want to spring into action; (2) I feel very strongly that I am supposed to make a certain choice or do something. I got reactions (1) and (2) about one of the cities and jobs. I believe that is the job I had manifested for Nanci and me.

Manifesting is not a word game. The phenomenal power to manifest what humans believe to be physical matter does not hinge on human language. Source has no language. Thus, there are no magic words needed for manifesting. At our spiritual level words are not even used and we are able to manifest instantly without them.

Manifesting does not require us to sit down with a pen and paper and write out our goals, desires, or wishes. It is helpful, however, to map out a plan for the "attention" part of the formula in order to more quickly and effectively position ourselves where we need to be in order to recognize our manifestation when it appears.

One reader asks: "Do I need to know exactly how to achieve my goal before I achieve it?" No. I have found since returning to this life that my conscious manifesting works best when I avoid trying to identify the way to achieve my goal. For example, instead of putting my attention and intention on shrinking my cancer tumors, I got better results when I put my attention and intention on healing in general—however that might be achieved. The saying "God works in mysterious ways" is a good one to remember for this purpose. Our manifesting may work in a mysterious way, one which we might not fathom using our limited human thinking power.

We may not like what we asked for in human words if we attempt to manifest specific events or experiences. That is because while we have a human animal perspective we are in the worst possible position to know what is good for us. Humans are extremely limited in their ability to appreciate all that is going on around them. They recognize very little of the ripple effect of their own actions. Humans have no ability to understand what transpires at a spiritual level. So, while in human life, it is far better for us to manifest an outcome without specifying a human animal's idea of how best to achieve it.

Emotion is irrelevant to manifesting. Law of attraction books ask us to invest human emotion into visualizing what we want. There are no human mindsets or emotions involved in manifesting reality. The power is spiritual and has nothing whatsoever to do with these bodies we occupy. We have to get the human mind, emotions, and body *out of the way* in order to consciously manifest.

Investing human emotion into your manifesting can prove to be your undoing. Humans' primary emotion is fear. And often when we fear something we tend to give it more and more of our attention. If we then start to believe the feared event will happen, we may very well manifest it. For example, I had a friend who was convinced he was going to have a heart attack. He went from his family doctor to a cardiologist and then several more specialists, none of whom could find a thing wrong with his heart. Still, he insisted he was headed for a heart attack. A few years later he did in fact have a heart attack, even though he has no heart disease. My theory is that all the attention and belief he was giving his fear caused him to manifest it into reality. He believed his human fear was a certainty and, at the Light Being soul level, was completely unaware that he could simply stop believing that and prevent the heart attack.

We do not individually manifest the bodies we inhabit, or their physical, character, personality, or emotional traits. The core entity Source manifests human animals via the biological and evolutionary processes it imposed on physical matter when it created the universe. Therefore, I have had to tell all my readers who ask whether they can get thin or beautiful via conscious manifesting: no. Biology controls that. We do not manifest our host body as an extension or reflection of our spiritual self. Source also created the panoply of human character, personality, and emotional traits that are innate to humans and are uniform throughout the species.

One reader asked who is responsible in certain instances for positive physical results, the body or the Light Being soul:

> Take for example the case of someone who wants to be better looking. Suppose such a person were to go ahead and undergo a makeover. In what sense have they "manifested" a positive result? You state in your books that humans (in the absence of an LB inside them) cannot manifest. But surely a mere human could undergo a makeover and become better looking.[49]

Manifesting did not create the better appearance, human hands did that. Manifesting created a new experience, the opportunity for a makeover, so that the person would feel good-looking. The man who had the makeover changed something in his beliefs. Manifesting always follows beliefs. The person either unconsciously updated his beliefs about himself, or he consciously chose to have a makeover in an attempt to change his beliefs about himself via a new personal experience (see Chapter 6, Step 4.B). This change will then result in his manifesting more experiences that reinforce his new belief of being attractive.

Another reader asked me a series of questions about the nurse I manifested while in the afterlife. In that scenario I saw myself walking beside a nurse down a hospital corridor on my way to surgery. This was one of the three manifested environments I experienced in the afterlife. More to the point, my reader wanted to know whether we Light Beings can create real human bodies for ourselves and others when we manifest physical environments in the afterlife. The answer is yes and no. Yes, we can create the appearance of a physical body for ourselves that has identical properties to the one we experienced while on Earth. But no, these manifested bodies are not the same as those Source manifests within the physical matter universe and into which we Light Beings incarnate. The nurse I manifested was not a duplicate of one working in the hospital the day I died. Nor did the manifested nurse have a soul like the one on Earth. There was no loss of life or spirit of the nurse when I stopped manifesting her. There was merely the cessation of focusing my attention and intention. While we are in the afterlife, there is more fluidity between and among Source's thoughts and imaginings. Everyone is everywhere all the time within Source. Moreover, our manifestations in the afterlife are limited to our own experience. In other words, if there had been other souls around me in the afterlife when I manifested the nurse and the walk through the hospital, they would not have been able to see the nurse or hospital corridor. The situation is not like the one that allows all souls on earth to see the same manifestations created by All Those With An Interest In Earth.

We cannot manifest into the body we inhabit a new talent, such as playing the guitar, though we can manifest a way to learn how to play guitar through lessons and practice. We cannot manifest a prettier face, but we can manifest the opportunity to have plastic surgery or use makeup. We cannot manifest character traits for ourselves, like honesty, empathy, or self-sacrifice. But we can train our bodies to display behaviors of these traits because these traits do exist as part of our innate nature as Light Beings.

Conscious manifesting may require changing our lives. The biggest impediment to conscious manifesting is the all-too-human resistance to change. For example:

- We want to be thinner but still eat the same fattening foods.
- We want more money but not to work any harder for it.
- We want to be better looking but not to undergo a makeover.
- We want to receive unconditional love but still treat other people the same way we always have.

It is human nature to want to improve our lives without effort, but that attitude will not help us consciously manifest something into our present physical reality. Manifesting requires that we change our lives. Sometimes it even requires sacrifice before we can open a path to the experiences we seek.

In March 2015, I discovered that a man whom the police previously warned me had told his rape victim that he intended to "kill Nanci Danison" had moved within five blocks of my house. At the same time, I was trying to stop a Peeping Tom from staring in my back windows and scaring the daylights out of me. I tried everything I could think of to protect myself from both men without having to change my own life. The police were no help. I filed a claim against the Peeping Tom and won but he ignored the judgment. I knew I had to move, but I could not believe that I should allow these sick men to force me out of my home. Consequently, I could not manifest a change in my situation no matter how hard I tried or how clever my legal strategy. The longer I stayed entrenched in my home the sicker I got with high blood pressure. Finally, I accepted that nothing I could do would ever make these two mentally ill men behave. All I could do was run away from them. So I moved into a beautiful house

I manifested into my life by finding it entirely by accident. It was heartbreaking to give up my old home, which had been my refuge through so many traumas. But I feel safe in my new home and my blood pressure has come down. The bonus is my new neighbors look out for me, share with me, and offer me unconditional love and support. Though my initial actions made sense to me, the tactic of trying to find a solution that did not require a dramatic change in my life kept me in a holding pattern that prevented me from manifesting a happier life.

The lesson from this example is that sometimes we have to hurt for a while as we get ourselves out of a situation in which our beliefs keep us from consciously manifesting a happier life, and get ourselves into a better situation.

Readers sometimes ask me how to know whether they are on the right path in their lives. One way to know if you are moving in a more productive direction is if it becomes much easier to manifest happiness in your life. Try one (reversible) step in a new direction, give it time to produce results, and then see whether you feel like things are working out better for you. Then take the next step and watch again. If you feel happier, less stressed or lighter, it may be because the new direction is more in sync with your spiritual goals. Remember my two city job selecting story.

Practice makes perfect. The only way you are ever going to consciously manifest reality is if you believe that you can. You have to believe that you have the power as part of Source. You have to believe that you have the power to manifest the same way the core entity Source does. How do you convince yourself? The same way you convince yourself that you can do anything else in life: practice. Take the example of riding a bicycle. Someone holds the bike for you, you get on, and you pedal for a few feet. Then you fall over. Maybe you consider that a failure. But for three seconds you were riding the bike. That counts as a success. You can say to yourself: "I did it. I rode the bike." And you know that if you could do it for three seconds, you can do it for four. So you get back on the bike and ride it for four seconds before you fall over. You say to yourself: "If I can ride it for four seconds, I can ride it for five." Little by little you extend the amount of time you can ride the bike without falling over. You have then convinced yourself that you can ride a bike.

The same thing works with believing you can manifest physical reality. You start with trying to deliberately manifest a small thing, such as a good parking space at the mall. Then, when you see it come to fruition you say to yourself: "I did that." Then you try another little manifestation, like finding exactly what you want on sale, and you see it come into being. You say: "I did that, too." Maybe in between you will experience a million little things that you do not want and did not realize you unconsciously believed. This is just like falling off the bike. Remember you had two successful conscious manifestation experiences with the parking spot and sale item. So you say to yourself: "If I can manifest those two things, I can manifest something else." Every time you try to deliberately manifest something and you see it come to fruition, you will be building the belief that you have the power to create physical reality.

When and How to Consciously Manifest

When should you apply the "attention and intention" manifesting formula? Whenever you want. It is just that simple. There is no special time of day or place or emotional state that has any impact on your ability to consciously manifest your life.

How do you consciously manifest? Focus your spiritual attention and intention on creating real physical life events and experiences. There are no detailed steps or instructions for how to manifest. As a Light Being, you instinctively know how to use this power. Just trust yourself and let go of all elements of human control.

The only difficult part might be training your mind to focus and/or getting your body's mind and emotions out of the way. The best way I have found to get my body, and its thoughts, desires, and emotions, out of my way so that I can concentrate on manifesting is through meditation. Meditation positions us to use our innate Light Being ability to hold multiple simultaneous levels of awareness.

Guided meditations and meditations designed to relax your body will not work for this purpose.

You only need to separate two levels of awareness to start consciously manifesting. And you can accomplish this awareness split by using the "Power of Now" technique, as it is described in the first chapter of Eckhart Tolle's book of that title.[50] To prepare yourself to experience the Now, get comfortable somewhere quiet. Sit or lie down. Relax. Focus on your breathing, one breath at a time. In and out. Do not think words. Simply observe or feel your belly rising and falling. Let focusing on your breathing clear your mind of all words. Clear your mind of all thoughts. Every single thought, every single word must go. Make your mind completely still and empty. Then wait and watch. Soon, words will form involuntarily. Maybe you hear a dog barking outside and the words "dog barking" appear in your mind in your human voice. You were waiting quietly for something to happen, and it did. Words entered your mind. You saw them enter your mind. You heard them. You witnessed a thought happening. If you are the *witness*, who was the one who thought the words "dog barking"?

At the precise moment you objectively observe one of your body's thoughts you have achieved multiple simultaneous levels of awareness. You have separated yourself from the body and its mind. You became aware of your body thinking—by itself, without any input from you because you are very consciously just sitting there, quietly watching. Who does that make you, then? If you are the observer, the witness who watches a thought enter your body's mind that you know you did not consciously think, who are you? The answer is: *you are the Light Being soul inside the human animal.* And you have a mind that operates independently of the body. I learned by dying that "mind" does not exist in the brain, no matter what scientists say. If near-death and out-of-body experiences teach us nothing else, they demonstrate conclusively that mind can exist outside the body. In the "dog barking" situation the mind observing your human behavior of thinking is the part of Source that is you within the human body.

Push the thought "dog barking" back out of your awareness. Just forget it and send it away. Keep trying to make your mind a blank. While you are clearing your mind of all human thoughts, let go of all human control. Let go of your need to have the thing you want to manifest. Let go of your need to direct the form the manifestation will take. Let go of your emotional attachment to the manifestation. Let go of your fear. Let go of your body. Be simply a mind—an intelligence focused solely on itself.

During a moment while both human and soul minds are blank, turn your attention to what you want to manifest and mentally form the expectation that it will be created in the physical world of your life. That's it!

If you truly cannot get your human's mind out of the way by making it blank, there is an alternative that works, but not as quickly. You can occupy the body and its mind with tasks that require some degree of concentration at the human level but not at the soul level. Some people have told me that listening to music helps them manifest because it uplifts their mood. Another technique is to engage the body in repetitive motion such as rocking in a rocking chair, mowing the lawn, painting, cleaning, washing the dishes, showering, and any other activity that requires attention to motion but not real thought. These activities can help occupy the human mind long enough for you to ignore it and enter a meditative state.

All you need to do to consciously manifest is give your attention and intention as a soul to making it so. It may not be instantaneous. When I received the Knowings about manifesting, I was given no earth-time parameters within which I could reasonably expect to achieve my conscious manifestations. But I was told that we have to be on constant lookout for something new or different that might be the result of our conscious manifesting. It might not take the form we expected. It might not even be something we think we want at the moment. But if we take advantage of the opportunity it presents, we will enjoy a happier life.

Important Takeaways from Chapter 5

- Conscious manifesting requires attention. We must focus our mind and awareness on using this power and on what it is we want to change about our lives. This requires mental effort only.

- Conscious manifesting requires intention. We must form the intention within ourselves as Light Being souls to create physical reality for ourselves.

- We manifest into physical life those events and experiences that further our spiritual goals—the reason we chose to incarnate in the first place. We usually do not manifest human desires such as wealth, celebrity status, or other human cravings unless they are necessary to accomplish our spiritual goals. We generally manifest opportunities for experiences more than we manifest things.

- We do not manifest random thoughts. We do not manifest human thoughts at all. So it does not matter what words we use, or what emotion lies behind our thoughts, as language and emotion are irrelevant to the intellectual spiritual power of manifesting.

- Conscious manifesting may require changing our lives in order to take advantage of an opportunity we manifested for ourselves. We have to be ready and willing to watch for new or different elements in our lives to see whether they are our conscious manifestations, and then decide whether to act on them. Just because we consciously manifest an opportunity does not mean we have to take it.

6

Improve Your Unconscious Manifesting

KNOWINGS I RECEIVED IN THE AFTERLIFE CONvinced me that we Light Being souls manifest events into our humans' lives both consciously and unconsciously. We most often manifest unconsciously, in accordance with our deeply held beliefs about ourselves and human life. Therefore, learning how to consciously manifest specific opportunities and events is not enough. We must also learn how to change our unconscious manifesting in order to dramatically change our lives.

Religions and spiritual books and speakers have done us a great disservice by preaching that changing our lives requires little to no time and effort beyond mentally repeating prayers or visualizing what we want in life.

Religions urge us to pray for change—even dramatic change like miraculous healings and life-changing events. It sounds so easy. Just ask and you will receive. A simple request. Has that worked for you so far? Have you noticed that every once in a while it seems your prayers have been answered, but most of the time they have not? You may assume it is your own fault that your prayers are not answered. Or you may buy into the theory that God has a divine plan that does not include giving you what you prayed for. When prayer does not produce what you want, does that mean you did it wrong? Said the wrong words? Felt the wrong emotions? Thought the wrong thoughts? Lacked the requisite faith? You may wonder what is wrong with you that you cannot get your prayers answered like the church says you can. Do these doubts sound familiar to you? The faithful have been asking themselves these questions since before Moses was a twinkle in his father's eye. Does it really make sense to you that all you have to do to change your life is ask someone outside yourself to do it for you? Is that how you accomplished adapting from childhood to adulthood, graduating from schools, getting jobs, finding a spouse, and creating a family? You just asked God or the universe to make it so? No. You worked for it. You grew into it.

Spiritual belief systems, especially those that include a law of attraction model of wish fulfillment, advocate fantasizing and visualizing to attract what we want changed in our lives. *Think and Grow Rich!* is probably the source of the current law of attraction principle that no work is required to create your ideal world. Hill writes: "When you begin to THINK AND GROW RICH, you will observe that riches begin with a state of mind—with definiteness of purpose and with little or no hard work." He continued: "The steps call for no 'hard labor.' They call for no 'sacrifice.'"[51] Rhonda Byrne's *The Secret* disagrees slightly, but tries to make the work needed to attract what you want sound less onerous by calling it "inspired action." *The Secret* claims inspired action is effortless and feels wonderful if you are in tune with the flow of the universe. Law of attraction books remain popular because of these promises of a quick and easy fix. Have you fixed everything in your life by visualizing what you really want from life?

Think about it. How many times can you honestly say that you attracted material wealth or a change in your life by simply visualizing it in your mind—even with a lot of human emotion behind your desire? Are you able to draw sexual partners to you by merely coveting them? Does your bank account grow whenever you feel you have tuned your vibration to the vibration of wealth? Have you ever lost any weight by constantly repeating to yourself, "I am thin"? Is there any object in your house that came to you out of thin air, with no one having to pay for it? Once again, judging from the reader emails

I receive, believers in the law of attraction question what they have done wrong when the thing they want does not float to them from somewhere out in the universe. Worse, most law of attraction believers I know are positive they have attracted *bad* events and people into their lives, even though they cannot point to anything *good* acquired the same way.

Prayer and the law of attraction are enticing because they offer instant, effortless success. Humans have become "instant" addicts. They want everything instantly, like getting food by merely driving past a restaurant window, or getting information by simply speaking to, touching, or typing on a smartphone. Humans have also become "easy" addicts. Our bodies want everything to be dumbed down so that it is easy to understand and absorb. Have you noticed how many movies, TV shows, books, video games, and other media have been dumbed down to the lowest common denominator? How apps are constantly rewritten to make them easy enough for a small child to use? How words have been taken off many signs and replaced with pictures? Even the cash registers at McDonald's have pictures instead of words. Cars are being designed to make them easy to drive by the impaired. Humans have created societies where putting little effort into life is not only acceptable but desirable.

My time in the afterlife absorbing Universal Knowledge about human animal behavior informed me that all their beliefs are founded upon, and flow from, innate human traits and experiences rather than anything outside of humans, such as God or Source. I was told in no uncertain terms that Source designed humans to be lazy, resist change, and take no responsibility for the consequences of their own actions. These traits are shared with many other earth animals. And it is these traits that have enabled the notion that humans can attract or be granted improvements in their lives without putting any effort into it, without changing their attitudes or daily activities, and without taking any responsibility for creating the parts of their lives that make them unhappy. Does this sound realistic when everything else of value in your life must be earned through effort? Of course not.

We souls have to stop clinging to the idea of a quick and easy fix in order to manifest better lives for ourselves. We cannot sit back on our cushy habits, put our feet up on old attitudes, and expect anything to improve. Alcoholics Anonymous says: "Insanity is doing the same thing over and over again expecting different results." I say that doing the same thing over and over expecting different results is the typical human condition. You will have to "get over" being in a human body and start to think and act like the spiritual being that you are if you want something better than you have now. But what you give up in terms of instant and easy is far exceeded by what you gain in control over your life.

Taking the following steps will prepare you to both consciously and unconsciously manifest more of what you want to see in your life. Here is the starting point:

Step 1. You accept that you have to change the inaccurate beliefs that hinder your happiness.

Why? Because manifesting follows beliefs. *A crucially important principle of manifesting is that as a Light Being you manifest what you truly and deeply believe about yourself and life.* The thoughts of the body you inhabit have nothing to do with manifesting. Your own thoughts as a Light Being soul unrelated to your beliefs have nothing to do with it. Routine thoughts are ephemeral. Beliefs are bedrock. Only thoughts reflecting your beliefs as a Light Being soul matter when you engage your spiritual power from inside a human body to create physical matter. All of the books and lectures about how to improve your thoughts in order to improve your life may help your thinking, but they will not assist you to manifest a better world for yourself.

Manifesting turns beliefs into physical reality. This is why some NDErs temporarily manifest into their afterlife experience the same environments and conditions with which they are familiar on Earth. Those with religious beliefs may encounter religious icons. Those who expect beautiful music and gardens may manifest angelic symphonies and gorgeous landscapes. Near-death experience accounts differ in the details of what the Light Being souls see and hear because each soul manifests its own deeply held beliefs about heaven as well as the treatment the soul believes it deserves based on its human host's behavior. These personal beliefs often differ from those of other NDErs and from religious precepts.[52]

Unlike prayer and the law of attraction, manifesting always works. It is only by virtue of manifesting that our physical world and bodies even exist. Everything in the physical universe is manifested by Source and All Those With An Interest In Earth (the parts of Source that maintain the uniformity of the appearance of Earth).

Because we Light Being souls think we are human, we generally limit our manifestations to what we have observed of physical reality from inside our fleshy hosts. That narrow focus can be changed.

Take an example of wanting to escape from a building on fire. We are spiritually capable of manifesting a swimming pool in the precise space where a parking lot exists adjacent to the building, so that we can jump into the pool and be saved. If we chose to do this, with the cooperation of other Light Beings involved in the event, the parking lot would disappear from physical reality and the pool would appear. The swimming pool was not previously hidden from our vision—it simply did not exist prior to our manifesting it. Manifesting always follows beliefs. We souls inside humans do not believe we can create a swimming pool out of pure thought and plop it down where a parking lot used to be. While we inhabit humans, we believe as they do. So, our manifestations generally take a form acceptable to human belief systems. For example, we could manifest a hero to save us from the burning building. Humans believe in heroes and would accept the appearance of one as extraordinarily good luck. The hero could be a firefighter already on the scene or a brave passerby who can be interviewed and celebrated by the media. Thus, our manifestation will take into account the normal parameters of human life because we believe in those limits.

If we could untether ourselves from the belief that we are human, however, we could save ourselves from the fire by creating a purely manifested being (which some call angels) who is never seen again after rescuing us. Or we could miraculously be cocooned in a bubble that protects us from the fire and fumes. That is the power of conscious manifesting unhampered by human-based beliefs.

The same principles hold true for manifesting wealth. Because we Light Being souls believe we are human, we would need to create a believable reason how and why good experiences or new riches could come into our lives, and manifest experiences consistent with that belief before we would consciously or unconsciously manifest wealth. In other words, we would have to create an explanation for how we could achieve sudden wealth. Maybe we bought a lottery ticket and then manifested winning the Power Ball lottery. Maybe we gained an unexpected inheritance. Maybe we dug up hidden cans of gold coins in our backyard that we found using a metal detector and sold the coins on eBay. All of these are known and accepted human experiences. Manifesting creates a believable life experience, not just the sudden appearance of money, like a rabbit pulled out of a hat. But changing the belief that we are bound by human limitations would allow us to manifest both the rabbit and the hat out of thin air!

Many spiritual authors encourage us to make daily affirmations or positive statements about ourselves and life in an attempt to change our thoughts. Others tout the use of vision boards, making lists, or daydreaming about what we want our lives to be like. I was shown in the afterlife that simply repeating affirmations, prayers, good intentions, and the like does not change our beliefs about ourselves. Neither does repeatedly imagining what we want. But new experiences and new analysis do change our beliefs. Humans, and we souls inside them, believe primarily what we *experience firsthand.* Not what we have heard that contradicts our own experience. Not what we draw, write down, or make picture collages about. Like the animals we inhabit, we souls believe what resonates with us as familiar based on our own previous experience, including our early age experiences with religious, spiritual, and cultural indoctrination.

I learned in the afterlife that in order to change our belief about something while we are in a human we must either: (a) have a new, believable personal experience that changes our outlook on the subject; or (b) conduct an updated analysis of an existing situation or circumstance and come to a different conclusion. For example, someone with cancer may be convinced she will soon die from it—until she goes into remission and stays healthy for years. That would change her belief about both cancer and the length of her own life. A father who detests the idea of homosexuality may come to accept and believe it is normal for some men when he is confronted with a beloved son's same-sex choice of mate. Witnessing unconditional love between a son and a decent, likable man can change even the hardest-hearted belief. Similarly, a person convinced that losing a job is the worst thing that could happen to him can change that belief when he realizes that staying home with the kids is his greatest joy. He now views the firing in a new light and sees it as a wonderful opportunity. A wife who believes her husband is cheating on her can rereview the facts and figure out he is actually sneaking around to plan a surprise fortieth birthday party for her.

A delightful little book titled *Who Moved My Cheese?* by Spencer Johnson, MD,[53] will gently guide you into an understanding of how humans react to and resist change, especially changes in beliefs. It will inspire you to be more willing to change and to act from new beliefs. I highly recommend it to anyone who embarks on this journey of conscious manifesting.

Again, we manifest into physical reality what we Light Being souls truly and deeply believe about ourselves and about our place in the world. You must accept this as eternal truth if you want to learn to consciously manifest physical reality. *But, no matter what you believe, you will continue to manifest your own physical reality, unconsciously, moment-to-moment in accordance with those beliefs.* You unconsciously manifest many events and circumstances of the life you are presently living (not including those governed by the biology of human nature) based on beliefs you may not even know you hold. Those events and circumstances will not change until your beliefs do. You will not be able to consciously take control of your manifestations and redirect them to better outcomes for yourself unless you accept the ultimate reality that we Light Being characters within

Source's mind who currently inhabit manifested animals can literally create physical matter from pure Source thought Energy. You must believe you are Source, not the host animal you see in the mirror that is limited by physical senses and human mentality. You must believe you are not a separate being from your Creator, the Almighty that manifested the entire universe. We Light Being souls hold the power and control over our own lives ... *because we are Source.*

Most people think they know what they believe. But they have not employed enough introspection to know what lies deep down in their heart of hearts. That must change if you want to consciously manifest a new physical reality that makes you happy.

Step 2. You identify the beliefs you are manifesting into an unhappy life so you can change them.

We souls often think we know the extent and details of our belief system. We assume we know ourselves well. But do we? If you are insecure in your job or relationships, childhood beliefs are holding you back. If you cannot trust others, beliefs formed from past experience are damaging you in the present. And if you do not believe you are a powerful extension of Source's consciousness, you have formed opinions about yourself along the way that are false.

Most of the time, we are aware of what we *think* we believe. Or what we have been taught to believe. Or what we feel we should believe. But we might not know what we truly and deeply accept as our own personal truth about a subject until we delve into it, which requires introspection. We have to do the emotional and intellectual work of discovering what we believe unconsciously or subconsciously because those are the beliefs that generally influence the turning points in our lives. This introspection might require psychotherapy, talking things over with a good friend who will not judge, practicing regular meditation, or following a program designed to help us elicit unconscious beliefs using self-help tools like Focusing, The Presence Process, or some other method we have found that works for us.[54] There is no one method that works for everyone. So try one and move on to another if it does not work within a reasonable amount of time.

Many people resist self-analysis. I have heard the phrase "paralysis by analysis" used to justify this refusal to become self-aware. Some people fear what they will find out. Others intuitively know that facing a particular belief and accepting its falsity will result in dramatic changes in their lives, changes they do not want to make. For example, someone who drinks to excess may not want to admit to himself that his family is suffering the consequences of his drinking. He believes the alcohol is not a problem and he can handle everything in his life just fine. He does not want to look behind that false belief and see the true one: that he believes he is a failure on all fronts, so he might as well drink himself to death. He knows subconsciously that if he faced that true belief he would not only have to stop drinking but also detox, get therapy, and start rebuilding his life. That looks too formidable to face. But face it, and change it, he must. That is, if he wants to start manifesting better life events and circumstances based on a new belief that he is a survivor and a success at doing the hardest thing he might ever face in his life—getting sober.

Sometimes we experience something we think we would never have manifested for ourselves, such as pain and heartache. Much of this pain and turmoil is built into the human lifestyle and biology, and includes accidents, injury, illnesses, violence, greed, self-centeredness, and other aspects of human life we would prefer to avoid. We did not manifest these experiences as such; they are simply part of the package of incarnating into humans. Other types of suffering that we do unconsciously manifest may arise from beliefs of which we are unaware. For example, no one would voluntarily choose to be assaulted and beaten. Yet victims of domestic violence suffer this risk on a daily basis. Why? One reason, among many, may be that they accept the violence because they believe they deserve it for not being perfect in the abuser's eyes. Or they may have formed a belief in early childhood, when their entire world consisted of dysfunctional family life, that abuse is normal. Or, they may have chosen this lifestyle as the Light Being soul inside the human because it is part of the theme they are studying.

Shared Human Beliefs

There are a number of widespread, normal beliefs that are most likely holding you back from consciously and unconsciously manifesting a happier life that you can work on now to get started. The human race as a species was designed with some character traits that have given rise to shared beliefs about humans and their lives that generate quite a few of our troubling daily manifestations.

One such shared belief is: "It won't happen to me." Humans can see a harmful consequence result from a particular behavior a hundred times and still think they will not suffer the same consequence in they engage in the same behavior. Many people believe they can drink all the alcohol they want without gaining weight, acting inappropriately, getting cirrhosis of the liver or cancer, or destroying their marriages, no matter how many other unfortunate "alcoholics" (who "aren't like" them) they see or hear about. Some people believe they can eat all the fast food they want without becoming obese no matter how many research studies are published, or how many obese people they see out in the world, because it cannot happen to them. Too many people believe they can use cocaine or methamphetamine or oxycodone just when they really need it without becoming addicted, despite the massive public awareness campaign about the dangers of these addictive drugs. The "it can't happen to me" attitude and belief leads many poor souls who do not know any better to manifest opportunities to eat, drink, or use drugs, with the consequence of harming their host bodies. And, because human nature includes a character trait of failure to take responsibility for the consequences of one's own choices, we and our host bodies never see the correlation between behavior choices and unhappiness.

Another innate, but damaging, shared human attitude and belief is: "I won't get caught." Many Light Being souls, unaware that this is a dangerous human belief, manifest all kinds of risk-taking behavior opportunities and experiences, which then result in unhappy consequences and lives. Teenagers shoplift, businessmen line their own pockets with other people's money, parents fail to save for emergencies, priests have sex with minors, soldiers kill innocent civilians, and on and on. I know an attorney who believes he will not get caught filing false federal income tax returns and so does it without a second thought. I know four other attorneys who routinely lie to judges because, so far, they have not paid a price for doing it. "Good old boy" networks cover for each other so that no one in the clique gets caught doing something illegal or immoral. All these behaviors eventually have natural consequences that make human life unhappy not only for the person misbehaving, but for everyone around him.

"Everybody does it" is another shared human belief that results in a host of manifested opportunities to engage in harmful behavior. Try to spend five minutes on the Internet without seeing nasty postings. Try Christmas shopping at the last minute without someone shoving you, cutting in front of you in line, or stealing what you have in your hands because they want it too. Pull up to a four-way stop sign and look around to see whether anyone else is watching out to make sure they do not hit you. When I practiced law, I saw hospitals pay kickbacks to physicians to keep them on staff because other hospitals they competed with were doing it. This increases patients' bills and the costs to the overall healthcare and health insurance systems. But humans are herd animals and naturally do whatever the rest of the herd is doing. So many end up posting nasty words, being a shopping Grinch, ignoring other motorists, and breaking the law because everyone else is doing it. Unfortunately, both humans and souls inside them have to suffer the consequences when the herd does something harmful.

There are many other normal, generally accepted beliefs we learned in childhood that prevent us from fully utilizing our ability to consciously create physical reality. They include the following:

The belief that you are human. If you truly and deeply believe you are a human being limited to the physical and mental abilities scientists attribute to the species, you will manifest events that reinforce that belief. You must believe you are a powerful spiritual entity inside the body you inhabit, unlimited by physical senses and human mentality, and not the host animal you see in the mirror. *You must believe you are Source.* There are no magic words I can say that will help you change the belief that you are human. I was so convinced of my humanity that I had to die to change this belief. In my previous books I have tried my best to explain who and what we are in as much detail as my memories allow. I highly recommend reading *BACKWARDS: Returning to Our Source for Answers* and *BACKWARDS Beliefs: Revealing Eternal Truths Hidden in Religions* to give you the background, reasons, and impetus for accepting that you are the all-powerful Source itself.

Do not berate yourself if you cannot accept that you are God/Source. The very idea smacks of sacrilege for those who are religious. The concept seems totally far-fetched to many. Even the Light Beings in the afterlife are unaware that they are not actually individual spiritual beings, as I learned while I was among them. The truth that we are Source is normally not made available to us mental characters until we have completed all the phases of eternal life and are ready to end living in amnesia. Early in my 1994 afterlife experience I remembered that before incarnating into Nanci I had been completely reintegrated into the core of Source. I volunteered to come to Earth and incarnate into a human to perform a mission, like many other Light Beings did. In addition, at the very end of my 1994 afterlife visit I reawakened to the memory that I am Source. So I know this eternal truth from personal experience.

We have been thoroughly indoctrinated in the belief that we are human beings and that as such we possess souls, that is, spiritual components that leave the body at death and go to heaven. These beliefs are normal and natural for us Light Beings while we inhabit animal bodies because we generally do not know any better. But we do know better once we get out of the gravitational-like pull of human thinking. In the afterlife, we know that we incarnate into humans and that we are not ourselves human. We know there are two minds in one human body. Two personalities in one body. Two sets of emotions in one body. Two innate sets of character traits in one body. Two sets of innate powers and abilities. Only we who inhabit humans—Light Being soul parts of Source—can manifest anything. You may be asking yourself, how am I supposed to know which part of me is the soul? No specific part of you is the soul: *you* in your entirety are the soul of the human and you are part of Source. I have listed the major character traits of humans versus Light Beings in *BACKWARDS: Returning to Our Source for Answers* and in the *BACKWARDS Guidebook* to give some guidance on how the two personalities differ. In a nutshell, nearly everything about the person you think of as yourself, the individual you think of and identify with as yourself, belongs to the eternal Light Being that you are. Human animals have very limited personalities and traits.

The belief that only God/Source has the power to create physical matter. This belief is true. However, you *are* God/Source. You have the power to create because you are an aspect of Source's consciousness, a personality or character within its mind. You can create physical reality and physical matter now as Source did when it first imagined this universe. The only difference is in the degree or magnitude of manifesting power you have vis-à-vis the entire extent of Source's power. Unless you can accept these new truths, you will never consciously manifest reality.

The belief that science holds the answers. In my youth, I earned a Bachelor of Science degree in chemistry and biology, and a Bachelor of Arts degree in psychology. I was totally convinced that science held the answers to all things, including spiritual concepts. Imagine my surprise when I learned in the afterlife that human science is the very definition of thinking *inside* the box. Science creates the boxes with its theories and then conducts experiments to describe the insides of those boxes. Science is all about understanding manifestations, not eternal truth. I learned that science is a fear-based endeavor, based on the human need to control. Science seeks answers without acknowledging the existence of Source, the Creator of the physical matter scientists study.

I have found that many people believe a quantum physics theory of how the universe was created. There is nothing wrong with such a belief. However, it severely limits your thinking by excluding the Source of the physical world within which quantum mechanics operate. All philosophies that attempt to explain Creation via scientific principles fall short of the truth if they do not acknowledge Source as the starting point of the entire universe. I learned by witnessing the birth of the universe that Source created the scientific principles that govern it *after* it manifested physical matter. In other words, science is subservient to manifestation, not the other way around. More important, the laws of nature that govern the universe came directly from Source and are maintained by Source. They do not exist objectively, in their own right, any more than manifestations do.

Some of my readers send me information about various spiritual or philosophical writers who have their own theories of how the universe was created, or of what we truly are as spiritual beings. Some of these authors have had a transformative experience of one type or another and write to share what they learned, just as I have written about my afterlife experiences. Their writings are enriching and valuable because the various ways they express concepts may give us a different perspective and trigger our memories of Universal Knowledge. But none of the theories I have read or heard about mirror what I learned in the afterlife from Universal Knowledge. For example, I disagree with those authors who proclaim thoughts are light or energy. Light is merely how human eyes, with their limitations, perceive some forms of energy. To my knowledge, humans cannot see thoughts as light or anything else. Thoughts are not energy in the physical matter sense, though they are Source's mental Energy. Thoughts do not vibrate like physical energy may. Nor do thoughts have motion and direction. I have read books and seen YouTube videos that propose these theories, essentially imposing human observation of physical manifestations upon what is purely non-physical. Thinking is an aspect of consciousness, not manifested physical matter, and has no physical properties.

The belief that physical matter has objective reality. No matter how solid and touchable physical matter seems during human life, ultimately it is no more than Source's thoughts and imagination at the moment. It has no objective reality outside of Source. In other words, if Source would stop imagining a particular manifestation, it would disappear from the universe regardless of what humans and/or souls believe about physics. It is because this is true that you can personally change physical reality for yourself.

The belief that any aspect of the human body can assist with manifesting. Some of my readers ask me which human ability can be used to manifest. The answer is always: none of them. There is no human sense, ability, emotion, thought, or anything else that can assist souls to consciously manifest because manifesting is purely a spiritual power. Humans cannot manifest because they are themselves manifestations. The fact that humans can reproduce offspring that are also manifestations does not mean human bodies have manifesting power. Those offspring are the result of the core entity Source manifesting the biological processes that result in physical procreation. Asking a human to manifest is like asking a dream character to dream or a book character to write the next chapter. The only way our bodies and human minds can assist us to manifest is by getting out of our way. Only our attention and intention as parts of Source's consciousness can manifest physical matter and physical reality.

The human brain has nothing whatsoever to do with manifesting. Therefore, it does not matter whether we can access our hosts' brains at various sleep levels; or whether we set our manifesting intentions before bed; or whether we try to get our waking mind into alpha, theta, or delta wavelengths. We want the human brain out of our way when we manifest.

There are no magic words, such as phrasing your manifesting intention in the present tense, or stating your intention with gratitude, etc. Manifesting has nothing to do with human language, and we want human mental verbiage out of the way when we manifest.

No human emotion can boost our manifesting power. It does

not matter whether your body greatly desires something, deeply and passionately feels the intention, or pretends that the hoped-for manifestation has already arrived. Manifesting is a spiritual intellectual power. It only operates via our Light Being soul minds. No emotion is relevant, and we want all emotions, body and soul, out of the way when we manifest.

Mental visualization at the soul level, however, may help with manifesting, depending upon how it is used. Something I learned in the afterlife that directly contradicts law of attraction principles is that we should not decide in advance what and how we want to manifest. For example, if we decide that we want to manifest finding a new apartment, we may go out looking for the ideal apartment, search Apartments.com, or compile a list of everything we want to have in our new apartment. All of that prep work is good "attention" for the first part of the manifesting formula, discussed in detail in chapter 5. And it does not hurt to visualize what we want. However, if we set our hopes on manifesting a specific apartment we may end up getting it and finding out it does not suit us. As manifesting was explained to me in the afterlife, it is far better to intend to manifest a new home and allow the part of us still in the afterlife to guide us to the perfect choice taking all factors into consideration. Our vision is so limited while we inhabit these bodies that we souls are really not in a good position to know what is best for us. So we make a lot of poor choices.

Muscle testing, brain wave testing, and other attempts to use the body as a springboard for accessing the manifesting ability are doomed to failure because manifesting is not a power the body can access. Many spiritual authors have preached that human bodies can raise their frequencies to match that of their souls and thereby achieve the level of Light Being soul consciousness. This concept is firmly rooted in the belief that we are human beings and nothing more. I too believed this before I died. But now I know that the individuals, the personalities, the identities we recognize and hold dear as ourselves belong to Source, not the bodies we inhabit. My quarrel with these authors may be just a matter of semantics that is resolved when we take the false belief that we are human out of the equation. Perhaps these authors are saying that only the soul has spiritual powers and, because they do not know that we souls are Source's consciousness rather than human consciousness, they assume that the human can access the consciousness of its onboard soul by going within itself. Perhaps all that these authors and speakers are trying to do is to give us a way to access our spiritual powers. But souls are not part of the body. It is impossible for human manifestations to "go within" and achieve the Source self-awareness and consciousness that we Light Being souls represent. We souls can do this ourselves without any bodily assistance. We need to get the bodies we inhabit out of the way when we manifest.

There is nothing your body can do to assist with, much less take over, the act of manifesting physical reality. The only contributions your body can make to your *preparations* for consciously manifesting are (a) human eyes and ears can receive information (for example, by reading this book) that may awaken you to a better understanding of who and what you truly are; and (b) the ability to feel bodily sensations and emotions can help you identify your hidden beliefs.

Nearly all of your spiritual beliefs are Light Being soul beliefs. Spiritual and religious beliefs do not exist at the unconscious or subconscious levels of human awareness because animals have no interest in spirituality or religion. Rather, spirituality and religion are Light Being interests that exist at levels of awareness we souls possess but rarely access.[55] Humans also experience varying levels of awareness, such as the diminished consciousness we see as the result of a head injury or during sleep. But those human awareness levels contribute nothing to your beliefs about anything except how the body functions under certain circumstances. You have formed the beliefs highlighted here in grey italics, and other important beliefs of your present life, the beliefs that guide your unconscious manifesting, using human life experience and observation because that is all you presently know. And you have formed them within the limitations and confines of human understanding because that is all you think you have to work with. Enlightenment allows you to see that you are not restricted to such narrow thinking.

Examples of Hindering Beliefs

There are many prevalent beliefs shared within specific cultures or across humankind that result in unconscious manifesting of events that make us and others unhappy. Some beliefs, such as those listed below, result from observations of human behavior and therefore appear to be completely valid. It is very difficult, then, to change these beliefs because personal experience proves them to be true. What the believer does not understand is that humans have selective observational skills. Humans are designed to be on guard for danger and focus in on those things and events they perceive as a threat to them or society in general. Humans also tunnel their vision in order to confirm what they already believe because that gives them a sense of safety. This is a normal part of the survival instinct that hinders harmony in our world. Examples of such hindering beliefs are:

- A closet racist will generally manifest situation after situation that he interprets as proof that his race is superior to others. Changing this belief will allow this man to stop hating his fellow man, to change his relationships with people of other races, and to open up to seeing abilities and virtues in people of different ethnic backgrounds that he had previously ignored. And it will result in his manifesting far fewer racist interactions and observations.

- A secret sexist will generally manifest situation after situation that he interprets as proof that men are superior to women. Changing this belief will allow this man to stop being condescending and abusive to women, to change the dynamic within his marriage and with his children, and to open up to seeing abilities and virtues in women he has previously overlooked. The result will be he will manifest far fewer situations in which he hurts women with his sexist comments and attitudes.

- A person who believes that alcoholism is a lack of self-discipline and a moral failure can learn that it is a medical condition shared by millions of people who are otherwise quite in control of their behaviors. The change in beliefs will result in the formerly biased person manifesting and responding to fewer incidents that she interprets as proof that drinking is a moral failure, which will improve her relationships with those who suffer addictions. It will knock that "I'm superior" chip off the person's shoulder and allow her to feel more sympathy and compassion.

- A poverty-stricken child may believe that only rich kids have opportunities in life and so manifests situations over and over again that he interprets as having chances in life foreclosed to him. This child may end up in a gang or on drugs. Changing that belief about who is eligible for opportunities in life can completely change the direction of this child's life because he will begin manifesting chances to succeed.

In addition to, or instead of, these commonly held hindering beliefs, we all have individual beliefs based on our personal experiences, some of which we have completely misinterpreted, that adversely affect how we manifest our lives. Here are some examples:

- A woman may have a conscious belief that males and females are equal and should be treated as equals in the workplace. However, she may have a hidden belief that men are all bad that is based on childhood memories of her mother complaining about men. In furtherance of this hidden belief, the woman may manifest incident after incident in the workplace that she interprets as men being bad and that she responds to inappropriately based on that belief. Changing this belief will reduce the number of times the woman might notice behavior she interprets as men being bad, which will greatly improve her behavior toward men in the workplace. It will also improve her job performance and happiness with this part of her life.

- A man who observed his father hating his job and grumbling about it every day of his life may have a hidden belief that everyone is supposed to feel that way about their job. It is normal—to this man. So the man fails to get himself out of a job he hates and keeps manifesting reasons to stay and complain. If he changed this belief he might well manifest a job he loves and thereby tremendously improve his own and his family's lives.

- A child who experienced severe food and clothing deprivation may grow up with the belief that he is entitled to grab, even steal, whatever he feels he needs to survive in order to make up for the earlier trauma. He may then manifest multiple events in his life that he believes can be handled only by dishonesty. These events are all tainted by his belief that he is entitled to more. As a child he may have cheated his way through school thinking his teachers were repeatedly grading his work too harshly. As a man, he may manifest opportunities where he can take credit for other people's efforts at work or embezzle from his employer. His personal relationships will be filled with situations he manifests to allow him to use dishonesty to fulfill his needs, like lying to his wife about his whereabouts so he can have an affair. Changing this core hindering belief will primarily improve the lives of everyone around this man. But it may also take the pressure off him to constantly try to get more by hook or by crook.

- Someone might have a hidden belief from childhood that he is not good enough for his job, wife, social standing, etc. So he will manifest experiences that confirm that belief, such as getting demoted, losing his wife to another man, or having to file bankruptcy. Changing this core belief will change the course of this person's life.

- A person traumatized in childhood by his parents' betrayal via neglect or verbal abuse may grow into an adult who believes there are threats to his security or welfare where other people see no such threat. To this man, when his boss says, "Come to the break room. We're celebrating Bob's promotion with cake," he hears: "You are a worthless schmuck and I'm rubbing your nose in the fact that you didn't get the promotion." Similarly, this poor abused man manifests threats, insults, condescension, and cruelty into many innocent settings. If he could change his core belief that everyone is out to get him, he could then manifest a happier life free of the need to constantly be on guard.

Any belief about life or your place in it that holds you back from manifesting happiness into your experiences can be changed once you identify it. Note that none of these examples is about getting a new car, new house, money, jewelry, or other items of material wealth. We souls rarely manifest such things directly, but may indirectly get them via manifesting that coincidentally affects our income stream. Also note that because other people are involved in our unhappy events, the cooperation of the souls inside them is enlisted at the spiritual level to join in the manifestation.

How do you know if you have unhealthy beliefs that hinder you from manifesting a happier life? We all do. I have read law of attraction authors who claim that emotions are an indicator of whether your body and soul beliefs are in harmony, or whether your thoughts match the vibration of an object or circumstance you want. These authors claim you will feel discord or negative emotions when you are not in harmony. I believed this before I died and always tried to get myself into sync with "the flow of the universe"—whatever that means! Then I learned in the afterlife that we souls generally get our thoughts and beliefs from human experience. Therefore, most of our human and soul thoughts and beliefs are already in sync and we feel no discord at all. Rather, we feel discomfort only when we try to change our beliefs from what we have learned through human life. New thoughts and beliefs discombobulate us because humans are Source-designed to resist change and we feel what our bodies feel.

How to Identify Hindering Beliefs

There are a few techniques I know that help identify beliefs we currently hold just outside our present awareness but which are affecting our manifesting. Again, we must know our hidden beliefs before we can change them and start to unconsciously manifest from healthier beliefs. This is the one situation where our bodies can help us by giving us feedback in the form of physical symptoms or emotional responses, as indicated below. The techniques described here are only a few of the many that may help you identify hidden beliefs that adversely affect your relationships and, therefore, your life. With each technique, you must start with a specific topic of distress. For example, perhaps you have a bad relationship with your mother-in-law, or your boss, or a co-worker. Work the technique centered on learning what you truly and deeply believe about yourself or the other person in the relationship or perhaps about relationships in general.

Focusing. *Focusing* is the name of a book and a healing technique developed in the late 1970s by Professor Eugene Gendlin, PhD, and his colleagues in the Psychology Department of the University of Chicago. The technique is specifically designed to heal emotional trauma by identifying hidden feelings and beliefs that are causing physical distress. Focusing is done by asking your body to give you signs about what is wrong. Focusing can be done alone, with a partner, or with a trained Focusing therapist. The entire process is fully described in the book *Focusing*, which is very short and can easily be read in one sitting. The most important aspect of the process is maintaining an objective, witnessing perspective as a Light Being soul communicating with the separate being that is your body. Basically, either you or someone else asks your body to give signs and symptoms about what is wrong, or what is keeping it from feeling good right now. You then take an inventory of physical complaints, such as pain, tightness, fatigue, etc. You select one complaint and try to observe it objectively without emotionally experiencing it. You find a word that fits how the pain feels, such as squeezing, ripping, or having a dagger stuck in you. As you say the descriptive word out loud, you observe whether the word resonates with your body, which is signaled by a change in physical sensations, such as the pain may move, or lessen, or change its nature. Keep asking descriptive words until you get a physical response to one. You then ask whether there is an emotional component to the pain by asking your body, "Does your discomfort relate to your mother-in-law [boss, colleague, etc.]?" Then wait to see if the physical sensation changes. If so, ask: "What is it about your mother-in-law [boss, colleague, etc.] that makes you feel so bad? Is it that she treats you like you are an idiot? Or butts into your business? Or second-guesses everything you do?" Make one guess after another until your body responds to one of them by changing sensations. This tells you what you believe about your mother-in-law or other person at gut level. It alerts you to a hidden belief that is poisoning your relationship. You can then decide whether you want to work to change that belief in order to remove the distress from the relationship.

Asking "Why?" Sometimes hidden beliefs can be identified by having a close friend, or even a stranger, repeatedly question you about why a particular thing bothers you, or why you believe what you believe about a particular topic. You can do it alone if you can be objective and honest with yourself, if you can maintain an intellectual detachment that allows you to observe yourself without judgment. Digging deeper into what you presently understand about a topic, and why you believe as you do, can often reveal that the belief is based on assumptions you made as a child but no longer accept. Take the example of a couple constantly arguing about whether their children should be forced to go to church. Maybe you are the one objecting to your children's church attendance, making every excuse and argument you can think of to support your position. The argument is creating conflict not only with your spouse but with your children, who feel caught in the middle. If someone were to ask you repeatedly "Why?" as you explain your reasons for not wanting your children to go to church, you may gradually discover that your own parents forced you to go to church against your will and you developed a belief that only bad parents would behave that way. You do not want to be a bad parent, so you refuse to force your children to go to church. But maybe now you understand that your parents were not bad, just religious. They wanted to share their life-enriching values with you. You can change your belief and behavior by seeing the situation in a new light.

Talk Therapy. Talk therapy is any technique in which a person encourages you to talk about things that bother you so that you can discover how you really feel about them. It may be most effectively done by a trained therapist, but can also work well in the hands of a clergyman or teacher. The person in the therapist role asks you to explain your feelings about a certain subject until you eventually come to an "aha!" moment and realize which belief or assumption formed the basis for your response to the topic.

Undoubtedly there are many more techniques for discovering one's hidden beliefs. Find one that works for you and stick with it.

Because manifesting turns your deeply held beliefs into physical reality, until you know what those beliefs are, you cannot change what you unconsciously manifest. Once you know what you truly believe, you can change false beliefs that are doing you a disservice. Then you can start manifesting from a better platform. You can perform what humans call miracles, like healing yourself from a terminal illness and saving yourself from certain pain, once you identify the hidden beliefs that are hindering you from manifesting a happier life.

Step 3. You have to recognize and own what you have been unconsciously manifesting.

It is human nature to want confirmation of what we already believe. Repetition gives comfort to creatures whose very existence feels threatened by change. Religions with fixed dogmas flourish because of this innate human trait. However, spiritual enlightenment requires opening ourselves up to new ideas and new ways of looking at the familiar. We have to be willing to consider the fact that our present beliefs might be the cause of our problems.

The only way to change the nature of most of your unconsious manifestations is to take ownership of them, identify the hidden beliefs driving them, and accept the truth that you create your own life based on your firmly held beliefs. Then change the beliefs generating unwanted unconscious manifestations. Take deliberate steps to create realities from your spiritual nature rather than human nature. There is a chart of human vs. Light Being character traits in *BACKWARDS: Returning to Our Source for Answers* that will help you identify your innate spiritual nature. A more extensive list was compiled during the workshop recorded on my *Soulless Humans* CD.

Your previous experience can make it hard for you to accept that you have been unconsciously manifesting your own life. We have a human habit of avoiding blame. How many times have we heard: "Sh-- happens" or "I'd have no luck at all if it weren't for bad luck." Or "It's your fault that …," or, "This is all your fault." We have all grown up with the belief that we are victims of circumstances. We all at one time or another believe that our lives are totally out of our control, or that we have no input into life's events, or that events happen around us without our foreknowledge or consent. One of my readers confided to me that he believes, like many of us do, that his life just happens to him:

> I can state that everything that was important to me or a turning point or a decisive person "just happened" or "was presented to me" for me to decide whether I go along with that or not. (I spare you examples.) I can't remember having had one single thought before that about the things and people that turned out valuable to me. I can't confirm that I seemed to have thought about a subject for some time and then—whammy—it finally manifested. In my experience some "higher force" pushes me in the direction it wants me to go and confronts me with the necessary crossroads.[56]

All of my reader's statements describe a life that is manifested completely unconsciously. My reader can recall no premeditation because his life is not governed by thoughts. It is governed by hidden beliefs. The Light Being soul is that "higher force," and it is manifesting from hidden beliefs that may or may not be serving it well in human life. Because we have marinated for years in human drives and thinking, we Light Being souls believe we are helpless to change anything about our lives. We passively accept as fact that life happens *to* us, rather than *because of* us. We do not remember that we have Source's power to manifest our own physical lives and reality. But we do. I was told this repeatedly in the afterlife.

Knowings informed me that human nature is designed by Source to include a character trait shared with all other animals: humans do not naturally take responsibility for the consequences of their own actions. You are never going to get a rabbit that eats your plants, or a dog that chews up your slippers, to recognize the consequences of those behaviors and stop doing them. Take the example of the dog that likes to chase cars. You can yell at him a million times not to run into the street, hold his collar so he cannot run, and put up an electric fence, and still, given the chance, the dog will run after cars until one hits him. Even then, the dog does not connect the car chasing to the injury. Humans are the same way. How else do you explain the woman who marries the known cheater or drug addict thinking, "Oh, he won't do that to *me*. He loves *me*." Unless something like the criminal justice system, parents, or another moral authority forces someone to, humans generally will not take responsibility for, or own up to, the consequences of their own choices. Humans generally do not make amends. They do not refrain from repeating bad behaviors. Humans have to be trained to behave well.

Part of the reason for animal, including human, irresponsibility is that most of the time animals do not *recognize* the consequences of their behavior, particularly if the consequences are removed in time. For example, if your dog pees on the carpet and you come home from work hours later and yell "bad dog!" your pet is not going to connect the yelling to the peeing. He is just going to be afraid of you and think you are crazy. The same is true for humans. Example: Sally tells her supervisor that her co-worker Sue is doing something against company policy. Sally has complained to management so many times before that she has gained a reputation for being a tattletale. When the supervisor reprimands Sue, Sue correctly assumes Sally is the one who squealed on her. So Sue yells at Sally, or tries to get even with her, days after Sally's tattling. Instead of recognizing Sue's anger as a foreseeable consequence of her own choice to tattle, Sally thinks Sue is crazy for being angry with her and that Sue is misbehaving.

We souls are just as blind to our bodies' behaviors. Take the example of a woman who constantly interrupts others and then complains bitterly about her daughter interrupting her. She fails to see that she does the same thing she condemns in her daughter. Or two people will get into an argument and one will yell at the other, "Stop yelling at me." And the other will yell back, "I'm not yelling." Neither one will realize they are both yelling. They will not even know who started shouting first.

If we Light Beings inside humans can be totally blind to our hosts' animal behaviors and their consequences, then how much easier is it for us to be blind to the fact that our incarnated lives consist of our own manifestations? Especially if those manifestations make us unhappy. No one wants to admit they are responsible for their own unhappiness. By failing to uncover our spiritual memories, we souls allow the amnesia of incarnation to rob us of the knowledge that we are part of a powerful spiritual entity capable of creating enough physical matter and other wonders to fill an entire universe. It is so easy to be oblivious—it is our default setting. And it is perfectly fine in Source's eyes for us to be oblivious; that is the purpose of the amnesia imposed on us at human birth. It is also perfectly fine to become aware of our power to manifest and to use it consciously.

Adopting human lack of awareness, we souls are also blind to the percentage of wonderful things in our physical lives versus the percentage of unhappy things. Humans tend to focus more on what they do not like about themselves and their lives to the neglect of the good things. So we too are unaware of what percentage of our humans' lives we spend being happy, or at least content, because we blow the bad times out of proportion. We must remember that we Light Being souls create all of the wonderful things in our lives as well as the problems. We may be able to cook, draw, paint, dance, sing, etc. These are all creative talents we have as Source, the wellspring of all creativity. The creative work we produce does not come "through" us—though we do of course use the human body to perform the tasks. It comes from us—as Source. We must take ownership of our creativity, and know that we ourselves are manifesting these wonders. *We* souls perform amazing acts of kindness that change others' lives. *We* souls manifest joy, achievement, fulfillment, and loving relationships into our lives. No one does it for us or to us.

We have to own up to the truth that *we* create our own human experiences. Not someone else. Not a god. We parts of Source manifest by agreement with other Light Being souls in order to create complex scenarios, but we souls can and do create some segments of our host bodies' lives. We each choose either to control our life or to allow human biology and innate animal traits to run it. It is possible for you to simply sit back and allow animal instincts and drives to control your life. That is perfectly acceptable because the only reason we incarnate into humans is to find out how they live and what it is like to be human. But we Light Being souls always make the decision about who is in charge. Life does not just happen to us.

Be forewarned: there are two potential human emotional downsides to believing and accepting that we manifest our own physical realities. These are human tendencies toward blame and guilt. You need to be prepared to deal with either or both. What I learned in the afterlife can help you.

Shortly after I entered the Light, my mind was inundated with Knowings about human nature versus my true spiritual nature. It was made crystal clear to me that I am not a human; I am what humans call the "soul" and I inhabit Nanci as a physical host for my own invisible mind and awareness. It was also made very clear to me that the personality I had always accepted as my identity—the character traits, emotions, loves, hates, memories, foibles—nearly all belonged to me, the spirit, and not to the body I had just left behind on earth. I was informed that we each have an eternal personality/identity that Source created to be uniquely ours and which endures over the course of the incarnation phase of eternal life and beyond. In other words, we are still ourselves when we incarnate into some creature or thing in the universe. In addition, the creature we inhabit may have its own character traits, emotions, thoughts, desires, and personality, like humans do. We combine our eternal personality with that of our physical host before birth and the amnesia of incarnation makes us believe it all belongs to the human we think we are. Knowings showed me that human animals have very little personality—no more than a dog, cat, or horse—and that Source designed innate character traits they all share. Humans age, but they never grow up. Only we souls mature emotionally. Humans live in the present moment. Only we souls ruminate over the present, past, and future. Just like other earth animals, humans are self-centered, selfish, violent, steeped in denial about the consequences of their own behavior, driven by appetites and pleasure-seeking, and lazy. We Light Being souls are generous, empathic, peace-loving, aware, driven by unconditional love, and dedicated to doing what benefits the most souls in any given situation. In short, humans are nothing like us souls. We can use this information from the afterlife to help us overcome both blame and guilt.

It is human nature to blame someone else—anyone else—for the natural consequences of one's own choices and behaviors. It is not, however, our Light Being nature. Once you acknowledge that you may have unconsciously been manifesting your human host's life, be prepared for your body to blame you for everything that happened that made him/her unhappy. You may feel an emotional tug-of-war between your body's need to blame and your own self-defense urges. It will present as switching back and forth from one feeling and attitude to the other. You may call it having conflicting emotions. The way I get through this battle is to apply liberal doses of unconditional love and compassion for my human host. I use the Knowings about human nature I received in the afterlife to remind myself that my body is doing what comes naturally for an animal. It is holding a self-protective grudge. I talk to my body as though she is a little child and assure her that I did not intentionally manifest anything to hurt either one of us. I remind her that some suffering results from illness, injury, poor choices on her part, and acting based on present emotion instead of taking the time to simmer down and reflect on better courses of action. I tell her that I did not know before I went into the afterlife that I even had the option of controlling her behavior to protect her from harm. And I promise Nanci that I will try harder to protect her in the future.

Similarly, because you have spent decades thinking like a human, you may have adopted the human tendency to blame your host body for all the pain it caused you by acting human. You could legitimately gripe about the body's excesses of alcohol, food, drugs, sex, and thrill-seeking in its pursuit of pleasure. You might accuse your body of dragging you through one emotional crisis after another, all of which you believe were caused by human nature. Again, work through this blame with unconditional love and acceptance of your body and its human limitations. Try to understand that limitations in human innate character traits and mental abilities may have caused some behaviors. Humans have a tremendous capacity for denial, which, when combined with living in the moment, can hide a multitude of sins from human awareness. Our bodies simply do not see that their own choices have generated the unhappy results.

Remember, you have always had the choice to either allow the body to act however it wants or to train it to act the way you want. Accept your unwitting responsibility for the suffering you could have avoided had you only known you can override human instincts and behaviors. Then forgive yourself because you, the small part of Source serving as a Light Being soul, are not the architect of the amnesia that prevents you from remembering the power of manifesting. You, as the entirety of Source, imposed amnesia upon the Light Being parts of yourself for a reason.

A psychologist friend told me to stop telling people that they manifest their own life events because it creates guilt for all the suffering they have endured and might plunge them into depression. I think the key to overcoming such a result is to focus on the facts. In general, no one intends to hurt himself, herself, or his/her body when taking an action that ends in painful consequences. For example, no one intends to kill someone in an automobile accident when driving drunk. No one intends to get HIV or HPV or herpes when spontaneously enjoying sex without protection. No one intends to tear apart two families when a spouse has an affair with another married person. No one intends to get hurt or to hurt the other person when they enter into a dating or significant relationship that falls apart. No one intends to get caught committing a crime. Humans, like other animals, simply act on impulses, drives, and appetites without considering the downsides of their actions. They do not intend the downsides, and sometimes do not even intend the conduct that results in those adverse consequences, such as drunken or drugged misbehavior. Guilt implies knowledge of wrongdoing. There is no such knowledge of wrongdoing in these situations because of human blindness to anything but its own current emotions and drives.

Moreover, we souls cannot hold ourselves responsible for the acts of our host bodies if (a) we have no idea that we exist separate from the humans we think we are; (b) we have no idea that we can control the bodies we inhabit; or (c) we fail to control conduct whose outcomes we cannot predict. Manifesting is complicated because most of it is done in concert with other Light Beings. While inside humans, we rarely know why we manifest a certain situation or experience. We may have done something that caused ourselves pain out of love for another soul. We Light Being souls are more than willing to suffer extreme physical or emotional pain during incarnation if it will help another Light Being soul in some way. So do not beat yourself up for manifesting situations or events that have made you or your host body unhappy. Simply concentrate on manifesting more consciously now.

Step 4. You can change body and soul beliefs:

A. by shifting perspective and seeing the facts in a different light.

Before I died, I had always believed that there is one right answer to every question. One true fact in every situation. One best opinion. And I always tried to find and hold the right answer and to do the right thing. I was startled to learn in the afterlife that there are a million right perspectives in every situation and that every perspective is the right one for the soul that holds it at the time the soul holds it. In other words, we are always right—to ourselves and no one else. The beauty of this eternal fact is that we can change our viewpoint, change our opinion, and still be right. And a million other souls with different viewpoints and opinions on the same matter will be just as right. The bottom line is that our opinions and viewpoints really do not matter all that much. They are flexible because Source is infinite and has an infinite number of different ways of looking at everything. I was told that all we need to do in order to change an erroneous belief about ourselves or life, and thus improve our manifesting, is change how we look at certain facts and come up with a new viewpoint and new opinion.

As an example, I had always believed the human myth that we are here in order to make a success of ourselves. I worked very, very hard to try to be successful in whatever I was doing and I often achieved recognition for my efforts. I studied and earned high grades in elementary and middle school. I was a National Merit Finalist in high school. I graduated magna cum laude with two science-based degrees in college. I gained a national reputation as a health lawyer in my career as an attorney with a prestigious law firm and have for years been named among the top five percent of lawyers in the country for my competence and ethics. I thought all of this was very important, using human standards of achievement. While I was in the Light, however, I was shown that all my efforts to be right and successful were really just playing out human fear. Fear of being wrong and losing self-respect. Fear of failure. Fear of sliding back into the insecurity and poverty that marked my life after my father died. I saw that this fear had tainted every aspect of my personality and behavior. Fear had corrupted my emotions to the extent that it was more important to me to work than to be loved. It was more important to me to earn money for my future than to show love to my friends and family. I was mortified while in the Light to learn that I had elevated into a guiding principle of my life what was shown to me there to be a character flaw. I dramatically changed my beliefs and behaviors in this regard after returning from heaven.

I was told by Knowings that we can use the fact that our viewpoints can change a million different ways to assist us to improve our manifesting while on earth. The power of a change in perspective is demonstrated by a simple optical illusion.

What do you see when you look at this picture? Do you see a vase or chalice? Look more closely. Do you see anything else? The image is called Rubin's Vase.

The shading in the color, adding greys and nearly black to certain parts of the image creates the impression of three dimensions, giving the vase a rounded appearance. The lighter grey touches are a reflection of light, which adds to the depth perception. Our eyes perceive a vase and label it as such. We believe what we see. So we judge this object to be a vase or chalice.

What happens if we shift our perspective with the aid of a change in the facts presented?

Now, what do you see when the shading is drained from the photo? Change the same image to white on a black background, and we perceive the profiles of male twins staring at each other, nose-to-nose.

Human perception is limited not only by what the eyes transmit to the brain as sensory data but by the human desire to identify and label everything as soon as recognition provides a word for it.

Note how your belief changes when you shift perspectives with the Rubin's Vase. At first you believed you were viewing a vase or chalice. You could only see the profiles of two men after shifting your perspective—the way you looked at the vase—from a 3D shaded version against a white background to a white vase on a black background. We can use the same technique to change our beliefs about life.

New information is generally needed to facilitate a perspective shift, like draining the shading from Rubin's Vase. For example, you may think your new neighbor is stuck-up or unfriendly because he never responds to your greetings. Then you find out he is deaf, and that knowledge changes your belief about him. Many of my readers think I am making a ton of money selling books, until they find out that I get no money at all from it because the publishing costs are so high. New information allows us to step back and see the old situation from a fresh perspective. We think it through, using our combined human/soul minds. We change our belief because we understand that it was erroneous in the first place due to incomplete information.

A technique you can use to shift viewpoints when faced with a situation that includes someone else is to put yourself in that person's shoes, so to speak. Parents know how to do this. They do it all the time with their children. Mothers and fathers know how their children think and can predict their behavior. Use the same method with other people. If you do not know the other person as well as your child, getting into her shoes may require assistance. You may have to ask the person to explain how she sees the situation and listen attentively to what she says. A good tool for determining whether you have understood another person correctly is to repeat back in your own words what you understood her to say. If you have already tried talking it through with the other person and still do not understand, or if for some reason you do not feel comfortable talking it through with her, ask someone you know who has good insight into human behavior to help you see through her eyes.

Psychologists use a technique to change perspective that consists of asking the patient to list as many possible alternative explanations for an action or comment as the patient can imagine. For example, I once had a very hard time understanding why the people who sold me my new house would not work with me to achieve an equitable resolution of my complaints about the quality of the repairs their contractor made to the house. I was very angry about it and did not want to feel that way. So, I wrote down every reason for the sellers' behavior that I could think of, from the benign to the offensive. My list included: the sellers acted out of habit, they were not taught better manners by their parents, they saw no benefit to themselves from cooperating with me, they did not want to fight with their contractor, they were busy with their new house and no longer had an interest in their old house, they were reenacting the behavior they encountered in the sellers of their new house, they lacked knowledge of how to do the repairs correctly, they have low performance standards for contractors, they were in a hurry, they are used to doing cosmetic changes rather than true repairs, they lacked money to do a better job, and other rationalizations. I had no idea whether even one of these excuses actually applied to the situation. But, once I saw there were possibly valid reasons for my sellers' behavior unrelated to me, I changed my belief that they were trying to breach the purchase contract. My sellers continued to ignore me and I had to spend a lot of money redoing repairs. But I did accomplish getting rid of my anger toward the sellers.

These techniques for shifting perspective can be applied to your own beliefs about anything and help you change those that are holding you back from manifesting a happier human life. We may not like what we learn about the beliefs we hold. But this self-awareness will help us broaden our understanding and focus us on beliefs that might need revision. I learned in the afterlife that humans have a huge capacity for denial. They can deny facts staring them right in the face.[57] So, it is very easy for them to deny personality traits and hurtful beliefs about themselves that are not always staring them down. Take the example of a woman who believes she is being helpful when she tries to manage everything in her children's lives. It may be very difficult for her to hear, much less accept, that she actually comes across as controlling and manipulative instead of helpful. But facing the false belief that controlling someone else's life helps that other person, and seeing that belief in a new light as human animal behavior, can free the woman from manifesting controlling experiences for herself and her children. A new belief is formed because the mother personally experienced a different way of looking at herself and the consequences to others of her former behavior. This new belief can be a springboard for new manifestations.

B. by having new life-changing experiences.

Once they get past early childhood indoctrination, humans generally believe what they personally experience over anything anyone else tells them. So, an easy way to change both body and soul beliefs is by having new experiences that provide firsthand knowledge that compels you to a new conclusion. The triggering event can be one dramatic unexpected experience, such as my 1994 afterlife visit during which I changed all my beliefs in one fell swoop. Or it can have a narrower focus, such as finding your wife in bed with another woman, which changes all your beliefs about her, and possibly yourself. The unexpected experience can be anything from an accident that injures you to winning the lottery and getting rich. We manifest these life-changing events with the cooperation of the Light Being souls inside the other humans involved in the event.

Spiritually transformative experiences can dramatically change entire belief systems. We have seen that in NDErs, out-of-body experiencers, and people who have been through regression hypnosis. There is no surefire way to trigger a spiritually transformative experience but we can pursue those techniques known to have spontaneously generated them in others, such as meditation, getting out-of-body, hypnosis, or anything else that allows us souls to break free from human thinking and beliefs. The information we gain through these types of experiences comes only from our own minds as Light Being souls, but it will feel very compelling and powerful compared to routine human thoughts.

Dramatic events are not necessary to change beliefs. When I practiced employment law I frequently encountered clients' employees who were certain they could do a better job of running the company than their bosses did—until they were promoted and found out how hard it really is. Remember President Donald Trump saying, "Nobody knew health care could be so complicated"? Becoming president sure changed his beliefs about how easy it was going to be to replace Obamacare. A do-it-yourselfer may believe it is easy to replace a gas water heater and that any dimwit can do it, until the one he installs backdrafts exhaust fumes and sets off a carbon monoxide alarm. And teenagers usually believe it is easy to drive a car before they start drivers' education classes.

If you want to change your belief on a specific point, immerse yourself in new experiences that relate to that topic. One of them may open you up to a new perspective on the troublesome belief. For example, if you believe all religious people think they are better than you are, attend a church service in a congregation that holds pot luck dinners after services. Mingle with the congregants and see that they are friendly and welcoming. If you believe no one could possibly understand what you are going through, go to a support group that shares your problem and learn that they do understand. When you believe your parents do not trust you to know what is best for your life, share with them in detail how different your environment is than the one they grew up in and ask them how they would handle all the threats and challenges you face. Join a group that shares a specific interest with you, such as skiing, gaming, football, or cooking, and see whether interacting with them changes your belief that you are boring and no one will ever be interested in you. Go to a retreat in a beautiful location and maintain silence and contact with no one if you believe you cannot feel Source in your life.

Our beliefs may change over time as we accumulate more experience in a particular area of life. For example, a friend of mine gradually changed her beliefs from Christianity to atheism because of how many times she observed Christians doing terrible things to one another. She reasoned that if there really is a God, and he controls our lives in this manner, then he is not someone she wants to worship. One of my brothers became a racist after joining the Army and having a string of bad experiences with black men in the military. You may have changed your opinion, your beliefs, about someone after you have spent time getting to know him. First impressions are often completely wrong, though humans tend to believe them anyway.

Remember, life does not happen to us. We create our lives, either by hitting the default button or intentionally taking control. So we have it in our power to increase the number of opportunities to change our beliefs by deliberately having new experiences. Do something out of the ordinary, out of your routine. Go somewhere. Meet someone. Take life by the horns and find out whether you like going to the movies alone, or joining a club, or taking up a sport, or going out to dance. Find out what you can learn by doing something completely different. One of my readers laments that he is unattractive and no amount of following law of attraction principles has changed that. I told him to go to a salon and have a hair and clothes makeover. He was not happy about that advice, as you can imagine. But the results of that makeover could very well have changed my reader's beliefs about his looks.

C. *by remembering helpful events or knowledge.*

One of the powerful effects of psychotherapy is that it can bring up hidden memories that can cure our harmful beliefs. Take the example of 46-year old Sally who hates her mother because she gave Sally up for adoption when she was three years old. Sally has been terribly hurt by this her entire life and acts out severe abandonment issues in all her relationships. During talk therapy, Sally suddenly has a visual memory of seeing her mother crying and screaming and being physically pulled away from Sally by people holding her arms. Sally then remembers that a stranger was also holding her back from running to her mother. This memory of a tearful parting between Sally and her mother restores Sally's belief that her mother did love her despite having to give her up for adoption. It also changes Sally's core belief that she is so unlovable that her mother left her.

Other types of memories can be just as powerful in triggering a change in beliefs, including spiritual memories of truths we knew in the afterlife before incarnation. That is why I have written five books. Most of what I learned in the afterlife through experience and receiving Knowings was very new to me. It contradicted my lifelong Catholic beliefs. But, emotionally and intellectually, I knew it was right. I knew it was accurate in my heart of hearts. I believed it instantly because I remembered knowing it all before incarnating into Nanci. My books are therefore designed to be a catalyst to help you too remember Universal Knowledge you had in the afterlife before incarnation.

Many spiritual authors speak of enlightenment and offer various ways to become enlightened with spiritual knowledge. We can read books, watch videos, listen to CDs or MP3s, watch TV or shows on the Internet, hear a live speaker, and listen to radio shows or podcasts to gain enlightenment on many different spiritual topics. Any of these resources can be valuable whether or not the content is true because the wording may trigger a spontaneous memory of eternal truths we had before incarnating. We know when that happens because we say to ourselves, "that rings a bell." The information will resonate with us. Sound familiar. Feel right. The new information may suddenly click into place with all of our other beliefs and make us feel whole and validated. We mentally settle into a new sense of rightness or security. We feel like we *know*. Recalling a powerful eternal memory about life or Source or ourselves can dramatically change our beliefs very quickly.

D. *by reeducating yourself.*

Most of our current beliefs were formed in childhood, some before birth. I learned in the afterlife that we Light Being souls are aware of our surroundings before birth. We hear what our parents say about life and about us, and we adopt those statements as our beliefs about ourselves. We hear what other people say they believe. And we adopt their beliefs as our own. We Light Being souls are at the mercy of those around us for a long time after we incarnate. We absorb family, religious, and cultural values through exposure and training. Formal education fills us with beliefs about how things work and what has been acceptable human behavior throughout history. We tender bodies/souls believe everything we hear because we have nothing with which to compare it, and, because our bodies instinctively love and trust everyone upon whom they depend for survival.

A few of us are force-fed different beliefs through indoctrination. Think of how cults brainwash their members. Consider military training and how it can dehumanize the act of killing. And remember that bullies and abusers can so overwhelm a sensitive person that she destroys her own sense of self-worth and believes the bullies' taunts. Indoctrination in religious precepts is often believed to benefit people by sculpting their beliefs about life and the afterlife. On-the-job training, trade schools, and professional training all use indoctrination to create beliefs in the material being taught and the trainee's or student's ability to do the work.

Anything that opens our minds to new ideas has the potential to change our beliefs. Reading. Seminars. The Internet. TV. Audios. Videos. Music. We can knowingly and unknowingly change our beliefs and adopt new ones through all kinds of formal and informal education. If you believe your religion is the only source of truth, take a course on comparative religions and find out what other religions have in common with yours, how they split off from one another, and how they originated. If you believe the Bible, read about how many different Bibles were created early on in the Christian church's formation, how they were constructed, and how the one you hold dear compares to the other versions.

In sum, if you are not manifesting consciously, you are manifesting unconsciously. You are always manifesting physical reality because it is your nature as a Light Being, as Source. *Always.* When you are not consciously thinking about doing it, you are still manifesting reality. And you are doing it based upon your unconscious beliefs. You are creating a life out of all the fears, hurts, disappointments, and expectations that nothing will ever change that you carry around in your emotional baggage. Or you are manifesting your human host's beliefs that you have adopted. Or you are simply choosing to allow your host to experience animal life without much input or guidance from you. But you have the power to change all that by changing your beliefs so that you begin manifesting from healthier ones.

Once you change the beliefs that have been holding you back, you can begin to consciously and unconsciously create a new reality based on your new beliefs about who you really are and are capable of achieving.

It is time to take control over your life.

Important Takeaways from Chapter 6

- Manifesting always creates experiences that conform to your beliefs about life and your place within it. Therefore, it is crucial to change erroneous or outdated beliefs that hinder your life.

- There are many beliefs we hold in common with others, or that we hold individually, that prevent us from manifesting the happiness we seek in life.
- You can identify hidden beliefs through an honest self-analysis, using a variety of introspection tools.
- You must accept the fact that you are the one who has been creating the discord in your life through unconsciously manifesting experiences that validate your erroneous or harmful beliefs.
- You can change beliefs that are not serving you well by shifting your perspective on a set of facts and seeing them with a different understanding, by having new experiences that will change your view of yourself and your place in the manifested world, by remembering eternal truths you knew before incarnation, or by pursuing formal or informal reeducation.

7

True Manifesting Stories

OUR MANIFESTATIONS MAY BE LARGE OR SMALL, temporary or permanent. Over the years, several of my readers have sent me true stories of their own manifestations with permission to use them to help illustrate manifesting principles.

In chapter 5, I cautioned that we have to keep our eyes and minds open to recognize our manifestations when we encounter them. We also have to be patient because we do not always manifest quickly when trapped in these bodies. Tom's watch story dramatizes both principles. In 1993, Tom fell in love with a Movado Museum watch he saw at the mall but could not afford to buy. He formed the intention to own one anyway. Four years later, while working as the lease return manager for a new car dealer, Tom encountered his manifestation while making sure all the cars and gates on the car lot were locked. Tom explains:

> I was walking between a row of cars and I saw something on the ground, but couldn't make out what it was because I only had a few dim parking lot lights. As I got closer, then stooped down to pick the object up, it was the exact Movado Museum watch I saw at the mall 4 years earlier. I was amazed because I couldn't imagine how someone could have lost this,

> and not known it. The band had broken on one end, but the watch was in amazing shape and worked just fine. The next morning I brought it to the [dealership] owner and told him where I had found it and I was sure the [watch] owner would come back for it because of its value. I sent a companywide email notifying everyone that the watch had been found, if they or a customer would describe it, the [dealership] owner and I would return it. We did this for 30 days and no one claimed it so the [dealership] owner gave his blessing for me to keep it. It's still my favorite watch and I have it to this day.[58]

To me, the best part of Tom's story is that he told me he recognized what others would call good luck as his own manifestation of physical reality. Your good luck is also the result of your conscious manifesting.

Tuula from Stockholm, Sweden, employed manifesting in a similar way to get a large diamond ring she had always wanted. She even saw and sensed this ring on her hand at one point! Tuula wanted to get married and had been Internet dating for a while when she found a man she thought she wanted to marry. Tuula describes her whirlwind courtship:

> It took about half a year when I got together with a man in Connecticut (via a contact site) who too was eager to get married. What happened was that he soon proposed to me and bought a lovely diamond ring for 6,000 dollars as a wedding present. We went together to the jewelry shop, so I was able to ask the jeweler to make the ring just the way I wanted it to be.
>
> This happened the year 2000 and the thing is we never got married. He found someone more interesting on the Internet, I suppose, and we separated. And

> I am truly happy for what happened, because now I understand that this man was not a person for me to be married with. But at the same time I am thankful for him. HE was the person who made my vision come true. I still have the ring. He did not want it back.[59]

Tuula's story shows that a particular manifestation may require two or more Light Being souls working together at the spiritual level to create a complicated joint experience. It also demonstrates the type of legwork "attention" that is sometimes needed for us souls to consciously manifest while incarnated. Tuula had to put in the effort to engage in Internet dating. She also had to be present in the moment during her dating adventures in order to recognize the opportunity to have the ring she had always wanted.

Catherine similarly used manifesting to find the storybook home she had dreamed about:

> Once I decided that I wanted to live in a little blue house with white trim and pink flowers all around. I began dating a man and when he drove me to his new house it was exactly what I had pictured. We married. It didn't work out but the house was perfect.[60]

You may call Catherine's experience a coincidence. If so, start looking for coincidences in your own life and you will find your conscious manifestations. Catherine later employed an "attention" tool familiar to law of attraction believers as part of her conscious manifesting. She writes:

> I decided to write an "order form" to God detailing the qualities I wanted in my next husband. I sat back and knew the right man would be sent to me. Dennis and I have been together since within 30 days of my writing the order form (which I still have) and we have been married since 2005. He is perfect for me

> and he says the same about me for him.[61]

Note that Catherine understood that she was manifesting these events when they happened. She did not actually believe there was an order-taking clerk somewhere in the universe, as some law of attraction authors claim. But her story shows that the attention part of the manifesting formula can be fulfilled using methods and tools you have used all your life.

Sometimes our manifestations take the form of opportunities to do something we wish we could do but find the roadblocks insurmountable. My reader Jean-Pierre tells of how in November 2006 he read an article about Haitians who were HIV-positive and could not take their medicine because they had no food. The medicine could not be taken on an empty stomach. Jean-Pierre was deeply touched and wanted to do something to help. But he did not know how he could get food to these poor people himself. Instead, he manifested an opportunity to help closer to home:

> The next day after lunch I was walking down the stairs in the parking garage. I hadn't noticed the woman who was sitting on one of the bottom steps. I suddenly heard a voice, "I am so hungry. Could you please buy me some food." The woman was black, maybe in her fifties, and very thin. I said, "Of course, let's go to the sandwich shop around the corner." As we were walking the short distance she said, "Please don't walk too fast. I have cancer and it hurts so bad." I said, "I'm sorry" and I slowed down. She said, "I have some medicine for my cancer that I have to take twice a day but I cannot take it on an empty stomach. I will eat half of the sandwich now with my medicine and save half of it for tonight."[62]

Jean-Pierre had manifested a way to help a needy person take her medicine without having to go to Haiti. This is the typical way we Light Being souls use our manifesting power, that is, to create opportunities for experiences.

One of my readers, Robert, told me the following story about how a famous author manifested a way to get her manuscript from a friend in Northern Scotland to her home in Canada without using any commercial carrier:

> On my first visit to the Findhorn Community in February, 1979, I was socializing one evening in the front parlor of the Community's large, stately old hotel, when one of the Findhorn members came through the parlour asking if anybody was going to Canada that week. I hesitantly put up my hand and said that I was going to Toronto on Friday, wondering what I was letting myself in for. He thrust a large parcel into my hands and said that this was the manuscript for [a famous person's] new (first) book and to be sure to get it to her by Saturday morning, because she had to have it back to the publisher by Monday morning. I said that I would be happy to deliver the manuscript to her on Saturday morning, but what would they have done if I had not been going to Toronto on Friday. He did not understand my question, because I <u>was</u> going to Toronto on Friday. I was the means by which their manifestation of the delivery was being fulfilled.[63]

The fact that the Findhorn member did not understand Robert's question is proof that expectation was the form of conscious intention he used to manifest this solution for his author friend. He fully expected that someone in the hotel would be going to Canada within the week and made it so with an agreement with Robert at the spiritual level.

We souls do occasionally manifest money for specific purposes, though we rarely manifest an entire lifetime of wealth. Mary Ann relates a manifestation where money entered her life in an unexpected, yet believable, way. She and her husband were living in a rented house near Palm Springs working from home in sales and marketing. Work started to slow down, and, of course, their income nose-dived, making it difficult to pay rent each month. Mary Ann writes:

> We had no savings to speak of and I was becoming increasingly distraught and anxious about what our future would become. So one day, as I was in a deep prayer and meditation I began to express my sorrow to my Source and I asked in all my sincerity if I could just somehow have a home of my own and more certainty and stability for our future. Not two days later, (I kid you not!) I received a call from my father, who, just out of the blue, told me he was sending me a check in the mail for $20,000 to use as a down payment to buy a house! I should tell you too, that my dad has never been one to offer money in the past, nor was he aware of my concerns as we are quite distant and speak only occasionally. That is not to say that he has not been generous in the past, as he has always helped me out of financial binds whenever I have had to resort to ask. But in this case I never asked him nor shared my financial concerns with him. So, somehow, my thoughts while in my meditative state where carried across the miles (he lived in a different state) and these thoughts were placed in his soul from this spiritual and universal thread. I truly believe this. So, we bought our house … and it manifested into reality, just like that, with no effort on my part other than the asking.[64]

Mary Ann's manifesting incorporated the element of prayer as part of the "attention" half of the manifesting formula. She completed the formula with the spiritual intention that she would have more stability in her future. Mary Ann tells us that she recognizes that the outcome was her own manifestation rather than an outside God answering her prayer.

Manifesting can make dramatic changes in our lives if we trust the part of ourselves still in the afterlife to guide us. Randy, a native New Yorker, tells how his belief in his ability to manifest a new future for himself led him to the famous spiritual community in Findhorn, Scotland. Randy had been working as a commercial film designer for seventeen years when that industry suddenly collapsed. He heard a voice in his head (not like a schizophrenic hears voices) telling him to go to Findhorn for one week in 1990, one month in 1991, and forever in 1992. That first week changed his belief in people and the possibility of living in a love-filled environment. He moved to Findhorn. In 1997, Randy heard another voice in his head telling him to build a Center for Beauty to be the birthplace of the next Golden Age. He was told that all the people and resources he would need would materialize. Randy describes how his manifestation took form:

> With nothing but buoyant enthusiasm, I started to speak of this, simply and without any expectation. Money started to arrive, land gifted, resources pouring forth, millions of supporters, a professional board of directors. Before I knew it, I had collected a quarter of a million pounds, without asking for anything!
>
> Crunch time came and I had to act. I approached the proposed builder and said, "I have one-third of the money necessary to build this center. How can we get started?" He responded, "Let's just begin and see how it goes." I was stunned. I had no idea of where I would quickly find a million pounds. I had dreams of my head on a pike and for 4 months awoke drenched in a cold sweat and experienced a nightmarish terror like being endlessly chased by a mad wolf. As an artist, I had none of the experience or skills to create a new civic building.
>
> Magically, our bank account filled to the level of

> just what we needed to meet each invoice of phased building. The builder himself donated 10,000 pounds to the project for which he was hired! Strangers walked in and handed over thousands of pounds, tours of the skeleton building brought in thousands of donations, people who had received messages in their sleep gave major donations.[65]

You can visit Randy's manifestation online and see for yourself how well he has done in consciously manifesting something spectacular for himself and others. Search for the Moray Art Centre in Findhorn, Scotland.

Manifesting can also be used for healing—our environment and ourselves. Stephanie tells a fascinating plant-healing story of manifesting that she and the man she was living with experienced together.

> One day, stressed out, I got in the "seiza" position (from my karate training) and began to do a typical karate-type meditation, clearing the mind, becoming simply present. In front of me was an ugly dying avocado plant that the man was trying (not too successfully) to make thrive. Because it was right in front of me, my eyes naturally fell upon it, and as I began to relax and set aside my daily stresses, I became mesmerized by the exquisite beauty of this plant. I could see how each leaf was perfectly constructed, was fascinated by the gradations of color, the very pores in the leaf. It was how everything that was created by "God" (I didn't use that word) was perfect, how you could cut it up and stomp on it, and still no matter how deep you looked into it, it would be perfect and beautiful, down to the last atom (or particle). I sat like this for almost an hour, just totally absorbed in this beautiful plant, and then I got up and went back into the kitchen to make supper.

> A little later the man with whom I was living came in. He went through the kitchen and into the next room, and did an about face and came back. "What did you do to that plant?" he asked. "I didn't do anything."
>
> I followed him back into the living room, and there was the most lush gorgeous plant. It seemed to have grown new leaves. It stood tall and vibrant.[66]

Unfortunately, after the man spent some time trying to figure out a logical explanation for the dramatic change in his plant, it began to fade. By the next evening it had returned to its former wilted state. I believe Stephanie's story demonstrates two dramatic aspects of conscious manifesting. First, we souls can and do change the physical matter around us. Second, our conscious manifestations may be apparent only in our tiny spot in the universe, and not to the world at large. The plant was lush and beautiful only while Stephanie engaged in conscious manifesting. Once she stopped giving her attention and intention to the plant's health it reverted back to its former physical state.

Important Takeaways from Chapter 7

- We often fail to recognize our manifestations because we label them "good luck," like Tom's good luck in finding the Movado Museum watch he always wanted.
- Our manifestations are often created in cooperation with other Light Beings inhabiting humans who play a part in the events we co-manifest.
- Our manifestations may take quite a bit of time, like Tom's watch, or very little time, like Catherine's order for the perfect man.
- Many of our manifestations take the form of opportunities to act, rather than acquiring an item of physical matter. Jean-

Pierre's story about helping the needy exemplifies this type of manifestation.

- Mary Ann's and Randy's stories of receiving money show that we manifest wealth in a form that makes sense to humans rather than money suddenly showing up in our bank accounts.

8
Manifesting Makes No Mistakes

FELLOW NEAR-DEATH EXPERIENCER MARY C. NEAL, MD, relates a charming story of a rescue she and her companions manifested.[67] Mary, then fifteen, was traveling remote Mexican mountains with adult missionaries and two other children when their decrepit truck slid onto the unpaved shoulder of the road. The group could not free the wheels from the muddy ruts, and it was too far to walk to get help. The road was rarely traveled, so a Good Samaritan seemed out of the question. As the group continued to leverage the wheels out of the mud, they collectively prayed that God would soon put rock under them—presumably so the wheels could get traction. The prayer was barely formed when the driver of a lost rusty old pickup truck came to their rescue. The group gratefully accepted the offer from the driver to ride to safety in the truck bed, on top of the man's cargo of rocks!

Some might think that the groups' rock manifesting intention got lost in the translation. That sitting on rocks in a truck bed was not what they intended to manifest. Dr. Neal, herself a devout Christian, believes God directly, though humorously, intervened in her life to rescue her. From the perspective I gained in the afterlife, however, this was a manifestation typical of how our manifesting power works while we are in these bodies. We manifest an unexpected experience that our human minds will accept as plausible good fortune.

Manifesting does not make mistakes. What might appear to be a mistake, as in Mary's story, actually reflects how we generally manifest physical matter while ensconced within it. The physical world follows biological and chemical rules that Source designed into the universe at Creation. We Light Beings inhabiting humans try to work within those rules when we can. It is far more likely that we souls would reroute a fellow traveler—with his permission at the spiritual level, of course—than create rocks out of thin air to bolster the wheels stuck in mud. Either way, the accident victims would have gotten rocks beneath them soon. But using the lost pickup driver is more congruent with human experience.

Source Understands What "I Don't Want" Means

Observant people unaware of how the manifesting phenomenon works can see that sometimes their manifestations do not match their literal intent. Of most concern are instances when the manifestation seems to be the opposite of what the person wants. Human logic, superstition, and the erroneous law of attraction have been employed to explain why this happens.

An NDE author I heard speak at a conference presented the audience with an entertaining description of the law of attraction. She said that the universe is like a giant warehouse from which you order what you want, just like from Amazon. She explained that, like Amazon's computers, the clerk in the universe's warehouse does not know what "not" means when used in an order. Both the Amazon computer and the universe's order clerk recognize only the word identifying an item in inventory. For example, if the order is "I do not want to get sick," according to this NDEr, the universe clerk does not know what "not" means and assumes you are ordering sickness, which she has in stock. The author recommends eliminating the words "I do not want" from one's vocabulary in order to avoid this unintended result. Failing that, she claims saying "cancel, reject" over and over will stop the universe clerk from sending you an order of illness.

While this NDEr's explanation is charming, it is misleading. There is no universe clerk. There is no warehouse of free physical matter out in the universe from which to choose. We moment-to-moment create our own physical matter lives in cooperation with other Light Beings. More important, we know the difference between what we want and what we do not want. We know what "do not want" means. And, inasmuch as we ourselves are the ones doing the manifesting, we are unlikely to get confused about it.

Napoleon Hill, in *Think and Grow Rich!,* may have originated the idea that God/Source/the universe cannot distinguish between what we want and what we do not want when granting our wishes. Mr. Hill coined the rule that wishes can never be expressed as a negative because, in the words of *The Secret*: "The law of attraction doesn't compute 'don't' or 'not' or 'no,' or any other words of negation."[68] Hill also stated that we translate into physical reality destructive thoughts if we concentrate on our lack of what we want:

> You will understand that the subconscious mind will translate into its *physical equivalent* a thought impulse of a negative or destructive nature just as readily as it will act upon thought impulses of a positive or constructive nature. This accounts for the strange phenomenon, which so many millions of people experience, referred to as "misfortune" or "bad luck."[69]

Hill correctly assumed that the same power that manifests constructive events in our lives likewise manifests destructive experiences. But he erroneously believed this power lay within the subconscious mind, and that it responded to an immutable law of creation called the law of attraction. Worse still, he thought random thought impulses could manifest. He called the physical mechanism for this cause and effect relationship the vibration of thought:

> However, if there is something that you desire that you currently do *not* have, and you put your attention upon your current state of *not having it,* then

> *Law of Attraction* will continue to match that *not having it* vibration, so you will continue to *not have that which you desire*. It is Law.[70]

Understandably, this erroneous theorizing appears in the Abraham-Hicks philosophy because Jerry Hicks taught the *Think and Grow Rich!* principles at seminars for twenty years. Rhonda Byrne's *The Secret*, written years later, goes a step further and claims that not only will you attract the lacking of what you want, but you will also attract more and more lack of it.

This logic is flawed even from the human perspective. All manifesting, all of Creation, is Source at work. The same God/Source that most religions claim to be All-Knowing is characterized by law of attraction proponents as unable to distinguish "want" from "don't want" when humans send their prayers skyward. Why would an All-Knowing God/Source be too stupid to understand "I don't want"?

If one thinks the manifested universe grants wishes, then it follows that the universe is sufficiently intelligent to understand human language well enough to respond by producing physical matter. But then why would the manifested universe be too stupid to distinguish what we do want from what we do not want? It appears some superstition has crept into the law of attraction theory via this idea.

Manifesting principles explain how and why we often get what we do not want. We manifest into physical reality what we truly and deeply believe. Simply wanting something—no matter how intensely felt—does not overcome a deep-seated belief that we do not deserve to have it, or an objective belief that it would be impossible for it to happen for us, or the mental depression that convinces us we are doomed to bad luck. These negative beliefs about ourselves and life are responsible for our manifesting the opposite of what we want, not a stupid God/Source or the universe.

We Mostly Manifest Boring Stuff

Most of our individual manifesting is unnoticed, undirected, and unimportant to us. We manifest all the little details of life that would bore us to tears if we paid any attention to them. We manifest the experiences of our civilized morning routines, taking a bath or shower, brushing our teeth, driving to work or taking the bus, doing our repetitive job tasks, and all the other events of our lives that are "nothing to write home about." This is not a mistake. Humans are designed to lead animal lives, most of which is repetitive and boring. I can readily accept that.

But, I learned in the afterlife that most of the events in our human lives are also unimportant from a spiritual standpoint. The only significant events are those that we incarnated to experience. Everything else is "filler," a concept I was quite indignant about when I first learned it. I had just spent my entire life as Nanci trying to make the *best* decisions, and to always do the *right thing*. I watched for omens to lead me. I prayed for guidance. I consulted psychics and psychologists on occasion. Before Nanci died in 1994, I really wanted to "get it right" because I did not want to come back to Earth ever again. Sound familiar? So you can imagine how distressed I was that most of what I had done as Nanci was trivial human life stuff. I had spent precious hours, days, weeks, and more agonizing over every major decision only to be told in the afterlife that it did not really matter which choice I made. More important, I learned that all the effort I had put into being a financial success had so warped my sense of self that I had lost sight of what was really important—loving other people and myself. If I had not been saturated with Source's unconditional love and acceptance while receiving these truths about myself, I do not know how I could have borne up under the impact to my self-esteem.

Remember, we manifest into physical reality what we truly and deeply believe about ourselves and life. Unless we have been awakened from the amnesia of birth, we Light Being souls are convinced we are human beings. We have no reason not to believe that. We look in the mirror and see a human staring back at us through our own eyes. We touch our bodies and feel human flesh. We hear a human voice when we speak. We experience the world from inside a body. For all our lives we have been shored up by the certainty that we are human. It should come as no surprise, then, that we believe the same things our animal bodies do. Our convictions have been formed using the sensory input of our hosts. Our philosophies are sculpted based on the character traits of our manifested physical partners. In short, we mostly operate from a human perspective—sometimes even when we manifest.

Does this mean human animals can manifest? No, not at all. Humans have no ability to manifest physical matter or physical reality. But we souls, who *can* manifest, are so greatly influenced by the human perspective that it colors how we exercise our spiritual powers.

When we reawaken in human bodies every morning, we have to reload our minds with human perspective and mental framework, similar to how start-up programs load on our computers. Our operating system consists of our human identity, including relationships, recognition of our surroundings, and our place in time and space. For example, *I'm Nanci Danison in my bed in my home and it's Tuesday March third.* We generally are not aware of these start-up programs loading and take this basic data for granted. You can confirm that this phenomenon takes place by recalling times when you woke up groggy, hung over, or in unfamiliar surroundings, and had to consciously figure out where you were and what day it was.

After our human start-up programs load, we begin mentally loading our working programs, like our schedule for the day and things we have to remember to do. One of the programs we do not realize we load is our conception of our world and life. Every morning we reload our beliefs about who and what we are, along with our beliefs about what the world looks like and holds for us. We do it from memory. We do it by habit. We rarely look at this data, much less change it. Consequently, we replicate day after day the same manifestations we unconsciously created at some forgotten time in our human host's past. This phenomenon is what causes most of the things in life we do not want. Manifesting has not made a mistake. We have—by choosing not to manifest consciously. By retaining musty old beliefs that do not serve us well. By choosing not to take control of our lives.

We Manifest Opportunities to Meet Our Spiritual Goals

One of the more earth-shattering, but freeing, revelations shared with me in the afterlife is that Source extended itself into little bundles of personality and self-awareness—us—simply in order to obtain firsthand experiential knowledge of the many states, situations, emotions, and sensations it can imagine. Source wants to live! Fully. Creatively. With total immersion into the virtual reality of physical life. It combines its intellectual understanding with its empirical data gathered in the physical universe to create what I call Universal Knowledge, from which Knowings download. That is why Knowings are so much deeper than mere book learning. Knowings convey the full firsthand understanding and emotional impact that only living through an event can produce.

We small parts of Source contribute to Source's Universal Knowledge by serving as its eyes, ears, arms, and legs in the physical world. We gather the experiential data that makes Knowings so rich. We each choose something about human life that interests us. Then we incarnate over and over again until we have satiated our curiosity or interest. Our course of study, so to speak, dictates some of what happens to us in human life because we manifest into physical reality the opportunities to observe something about what interests us. This may create repeating patterns in our lives because we want to see every single aspect and facet of what we are here to experience. This is not a manifesting mistake. We may have to manifest various versions of the same opportunity over and over again before we souls notice it and pursue it. That is why, I learned, it is impossible to fail at our goal of experiencing something that interests us about human life. We manifest the chance to understand the desired experience from as many perspectives as possible until we either complete our goal or decide it is impossible to do so in the human life we have chosen.

We Manifest Problems to Solve

Sometimes we Light Being souls notice that our hosts keep encountering the same problem or situation over and over again. It feels like a pox on our house. Once we realize that insanity is doing the same thing over and over again expecting different results, we change how we handle the problem or situation each time it recurs. We try everything we can think of to resolve the problem or situation in an attempt to keep it from repeating. Over and over, we ask ourselves, "What am I supposed to learn from this?" Surely, we think, there must be some meaning in the fact that the same problem or situation keeps coming into our lives. This is how the law of attraction hooks its believers. It gives us an explanation, albeit an irrational one. And we say, "Aha, I'm attracting this problem or situation to myself with my thoughts." Not true. This pattern in our lives is not a manifesting mistake. We are simply manifesting opportunities to meet our goal.

I am not saying that we are here on Earth to learn something, such as how to love or how to be a more spiritual person. I was indoctrinated in the afterlife that our purpose for incarnating is not to *learn* anything. As parts of Source we have unlimited access to everything it knows, what I call Universal Knowledge, and Source is All-Knowing. When we are in the afterlife all we have to do to know everything there is to know about any subject is to focus our attention on it with the intention to receive Knowings. There is nothing human life can teach us that we cannot learn instantly via accessing Universal Knowledge. We incarnate in order to know what it *feels* like to have our own unique experiences, including those we manifest in order to meet our own goals for coming here. We incarnate for the emotional content of life, not the knowledge content. We incarnate to challenge ourselves with new adventures just to see what they are like and how we handle them.

Most of the recurring events of our lives that present a challenge in one way or another are part of the experience package we signed up for when we chose to enter into human life. We manifest these situations ourselves simply in order to see how we handle them and/or resolve them. Perhaps in another physical lifetime we had a problem with being bullied. We may choose to manifest many bullying instances into our current lifetime to see whether we can divine a new way to stop it, accept it, or resolve it. We may manifest bullying (with the cooperation of other souls) just to see whether over a series of incarnations we have adopted a new way to handle human animal traits. Or to see whether we still get as upset about the problem or situation as in the past. Or to find out whether therapy is working. Or to test our resilience. Or any one of a hundred other reasons that make sense only to us Light Beings. We may never figure out during human life why we are doing this to ourselves. But our life review when we return to the afterlife will reveal all and show how the pieces fit together with our eternal life goals.

We Manifest Our Financial Circumstances

Remember: we manifest unconsciously most of the time. And *what* we manifest unconsciously is exactly what we have come to believe about the circumstances of our current human lifetime. If simple observation and personal experience demonstrate to us that we are not wealthy, we will truly and deeply believe we are not wealthy and will continue to manifest that lifestyle. All the self-talk and positive affirmations in the world are not going to convince you that you are rich if you can look out your window and see three generations of your family living in poverty. Humans believe what they personally experience through their senses, and we souls believe what our hosts believe.

But some poor people are able to rise above the obvious and believe they have abundance in one or more ways. These souls always seem to find that needed dollar or resource at the last minute because their belief that they are blessed and will be taken care of manifests into physical matter. I am one of those souls.

There have been many times in Nanci's life when I and my family have been very poor. But my mother taught me to believe that the poor souls in heaven would take care of us. Somebody always did. For instance, while I was in Catholic elementary school our parish would collect food to deliver to the poor families of the parish at Christmas. The year my father died, when my family was down to our last dollar, several men from the parish delivered many bags of groceries to us right before Christmas. I was mortified that after contributing to this parish project year after year while in elementary school, this year we were the poor family! But we were taken care of, just as I believed. Clearly I did not manifest wealth into my life in this instance. That is because I paid the bills and balanced the family checkbook for my mother and knew we were poor. I therefore truly and deeply believed that wealth was not part of my life.

Also during my childhood, I came to believe that I could earn money and take care of myself and my family like my father did before he died. I worked without interruption toward that goal from age thirteen, consistently manifesting various opportunities to work to support myself and my family.

Who Manifests Suffering?

The number one comment I receive from readers when I speak or write about manifesting is some form of, "There's no way you can convince me that I manifested this suffering for myself."

Humans, and by extention souls, are loath to accept responsibility for the consequences of their own behavior, and that feeling is magnified and compounded when the consequences cause suffering. Notwithstanding these all-too-human perspectives on the matter, I did learn in the afterlife that we manifest the content of our human lives *within the parameters of the laws of the physical universe set by Source*. In other words, if the laws of gravity, thermodynamics, biology, physics, and other sciences lead to a predictable result, we will experience that result even though we have not consciously or unconsciously manifested it. For example, if we lose control of a car we are driving, we will crash even though we do not intend to manifest an automobile accident. When we climb a mountain and lose our grip, we will fall to our death, though we never intended that. And, engaging in risky behaviors may result in serious unintended consequences simply as a matter of scientific laws. It is not your fault if you suffer an injury resulting from risky behavior because those injuries are the natural consequence of gravity and other forces. It is, however, your choice to take those risks. You do manifest into physical reality the opportunities to take risks. You did manifest into physical life the logistics of taking time off work, traveling to the Rockies, and joining an expedition to the top of the mountain from which you fell.

Some sources of suffering are built into the physical environment and the laws of nature that govern it. The "matrix," as it were, of the physical environment we all experience is generated by All Those With An Interest In Earth and is not the result of our own personal manifesting. We cannot individually change the weather for everyone around us. We cannot individually manifest a hurricane, a tsunami, or a volcanic eruption. Nor do we manifest the timing of natural disasters to correspond to anything in our individual lives. In other words, it is not your fault that your house got blown away by a tornado no matter how many times you wished you could tear it down and build a new one. You did not attract that tornado with your thoughts or manifest it.

Some causes of suffering are simply inconsiderate or negligent or unkind human behaviors. Someone does not filter her words, hurts a friend with them, and ends up losing the friend. A wife does not remember that her husband worked hard physically that day and drags him to a dinner party he does not want to attend. They end up in a fight that hurts them both. A farmer thinks only of his own yard being torn up when he goes after moles in their tunnels with a pitchfork. The moles escape into the neighboring yards, costing his neighbors a lot of aggravation and money. Politicians falsely accuse each other of heinous acts in political campaigns, resulting in very painful and irreparable damage to reputations and relationships, and still end up losing the office they sought. These events are part human animal nature playing out and part manifesting. How? Humans do not naturally filter their speech and a person's parental training might instill a belief that it is permissible to say unkind things if they are true, or when part of a political campaign. Humans are self-centered and controlling, believe that selfish behavior is acceptable, and that belief causes the wife and mole-killer to manifest events that meet their needs to the detriment of others. But, in the end, all these souls caused their own suffering by unconsciously manifesting from harmful human beliefs.

One of my readers commented to me with respect to a relative: "It's almost as if she's attracting back luck to herself." Sounds like Napoleon Hill's thinking. Neither humans nor Light Being souls attract bad or good luck. The idea that we are innocent bystanders pulling in bad luck like a magnet ignores the power we have as spiritual beings. We do not attract events into our lives from some outside supply of them. We create events through manifesting, even the painful ones. No one forces life's situations on us. And no one has it in for us on a cosmic level. There is no karma at work in our lives. No one controls our lives but us. So it behooves us to make more of an effort to heal our hindering beliefs so that our unconscious manifestations create a happier life. When we feel as though we are stuck in a run of bad luck, it is because we have been manifesting from unhealthy unconscious beliefs. Change the beliefs and you will change the experiences.

Important Takeaways from Chapter 8

- We make no mistakes in our manifesting. We may manifest experiences our bodies do not want. But everything we manifest into our human lives is intended because intention is half the manifesting formula.
- We manifest all the boring day-to-day events of our human lives mostly out of habit and based on unconscious beliefs we have accumulated over the years. All of these manifestations are available for change.
- We manifest many opportunities to meet our spiritual goals. If we do not choose one or more opportunities, we just manifest others until we do choose to act. There is no way we can miss fulfilling our spiritual goal.
- We manifest problems, crises, and pressure-cooker situations because we Light Beings love a challenge and we are curious about how we will handle each one.

- We manifest some of our suffering because we souls are simply following the beliefs we have picked up from humans. Other sources of suffering are built into the physical world experience.

9

Co-Creating

ALL OF CREATION IS THE RESULT OF SOURCE MANIfesting its imagination.

The core entity Source manifested the entire universe and all that is in it, everything humans consider to be physical matter reality, through the power of its imagination, attention, and intention. I learned in the afterlife that the ongoing responsibility for maintaining the manifestation of Earth, and everything on it, is delegated to a group of Source's mental characters that I call All Those With An Interest In Earth. This is a group of Light Being characters within Source's mind who at some point in their eternal lives incarnated into some type of physical matter on Earth, such as plants, animals, or things. They are responsible for the day-to-day maintenance of the physical matter manifestation that scientists study. We are included in this Light Being group. Each one of us souls currently inside a human does our part to preserve Earth's overall physical appearance and functioning. We Light Being souls are each *co-creators* of Earth, its biosphere and appearance, as parts of Source's thoughts and imagination.

Humans are also manifested. They have no substance outside the mind of Source. They are merely Source's imagination, similar to our dream characters. In other words, we souls do not individually manifest our own human body as our outward appearance in the physical world. Humans were not created the way that the Book of Genesis portrays it. I remember from watching Creation play out that humans evolved from what we consider to be lower-level life forms. Thus humans are manifested by the core entity Source via the evolutionary processes it built into Creation.

Source indirectly manifests every moment of human life in the sense that most human behavior and experiences are the result of the Source-created animal drives, instincts, emotions, innate character and species traits, and other aspects of human animals that contribute to behavior. The routine aspects of animal life, such as eating, drinking, sleeping, nesting, recreating, and procreating, are automatic. These are driven by the biological processes Source created and imposed upon its imaginary physical world. Therefore, Source does not directly manifest humans feeding themselves and their offspring any more than it directly manifests birds doing the same thing. Nor do we Light Being souls inside humans manifest the purely animal aspects of life for our hosts. In other words, although we souls may on occasion deliberately choose what foods our bodies will eat, and manifest opportunities to obtain that precise food, the act of eating is manifested via biological processes. Humans are alive and perfectly capable of enjoying their birth-to-death life span without any Light Being soul inside. Most of us souls simply go along for the ride inside humans and allow our bodies to live out their animal lives without much intervention from us. This accounts for most of the selfishness, self-centeredness, laziness, addictions, and violent behavior we observe every day.

We souls do, however, manifest non-animal day-to-day activities, as well as certain events needed to fulfill our reasons for incarnating. We manifest our beliefs about what human life should be like, which are borrowed from our human hosts, into our bodies' physical matter experiences. We manifest our human's and our own emotional problems into physical reality. We also manifest specific events in concert with the parts of us, our other levels of awareness, still in the afterlife that are helping us fulfill our spiritual goals. I wish I could give you a list of examples of what we souls manifest, but each life is so different. And I do not remember that level of detail from the Knowings on manifesting I was given in the afterlife. The memories simply did not survive being stuffed back into this body. I am sorry.

Like cats, dogs, horses, pigs, and other domesticated higher level animals, humans do not have any control over or input into the physical course of their own lives. They respond to chemical processes within their manifested bodies. Their animal activities result from manifested biological processes. In short, humans are like cars that can drive themselves, or smartphones that can talk to us. Source creates their lives either by keeping hands off and allowing biological processes to play out or by manifesting from inside humans through the efforts of Light Being souls. Note that creation of life's events does not equal control over them. Source does not control our behavior, or humans' behavior. Just the opposite. Source lets its imagination run wild through us and its manifestations.

On an individual soul basis, co-manifesting is a collaborative effort between the Light Being part of us inside the body and the part of us still in the afterlife. The part of us here has no idea what we are supposed to do. The part of us still in the afterlife, on the other hand, knows our goals and helps us achieve them through the power of co-creating or co-manifesting. Co-creating is also a collaborative effort between and among us working in groups of souls and working with Light Beings in the afterlife. We make agreements at the spiritual level to jointly experience a certain event or circumstance and manifest it together. I do not remember the details of how this all works. All I know is that our manifestations are a hodgepodge of the creative intentions of these many aspects of Source, all trying to accomplish Source's goal of experiencing all it can imagine.

We have loved ones in the afterlife, just as we do in human life, and we may decide to incarnate at the same time as some of our eternal friends. This group of souls will work together to manifest their interactions on earth. Similarly, if we agreed to incarnate with another Light Being we love in order to be a support person, or a catalyst for something they want to do, we will jointly manifest the supportive experiences or goal event or action.

Overlaying all that spiritual intention—working as the rudder giving us direction—are our personal belief systems, composed partly of memories of Universal Knowledge but mostly of human beliefs. Most of us do not realize that Source designed humans to have very limited senses. Nevertheless, along with our humans, we draw conclusions from and believe the limited data our bodies provide.

Manifesting is always collaborative within Source's mind. One of my readers once asked me: "If two people want the same thing [at the same time] and only one can have it, and both are able to manifest it, who gets it?[71] The wording of this question suggests to me that my reader is thinking like a competitive human.

My reader may be referring to manifesting an event or opportunity open to only one person, for which two humans are competing. If an event must go only one way or the other—such as being elected U.S. president or marrying a particular person—then a lot of factors come into play. First and foremost is the animal competition. Governing other humans and marriage are both animal behaviors. Both humans will use innate human character traits, like cunning and dishonesty, to one up each other. The one who more successfully uses animal traits to achieve the desired end will prevail. If, however, the election or marriage is integral to either soul's goal in human life, the parts of the two Light Beings still in the afterlife will work out an agreement and manifest that agreed-upon solution together. Often the agreement will give both parties some or all of what they want—perhaps the same opportunity or event sequentially over time, or in a different form than the human hosts envisioned. For example, one person might be elected president this term, followed by the other person in another election. Or both will become Leaders of their parties in the Senate, also a very powerful position. Or the competing humans will marry the same person sequentially. None of this soul intervention into animal behavior will happen, of course, unless it furthers the two souls' spiritual goals.

"What if they both believe 100 percent that they will get it? Then who gets it?"[72] my reader asks. Belief at the human level of awareness is irrelevant because humans cannot manifest their beliefs into physical reality. If the event is irrelevant to either soul's incarnation goals, the better animal competitor will get it. If the event does further one or both souls' spiritual goals, then only the involved Light Being souls' intentions matter, and those will be collaborative rather than competitive. If, however, each person's belief that he will get the thing exists at the soul level, and the expectation meets the intention requirement, the result may be a tie, someone else entirely gets it, or each person gets it but at different times, as in the example of being elected president. There is no "time" outside these bodies. So, manifesting does not follow a human timetable.

We manifest physical reality all the time. Alone and with other Light Beings/souls we create opportunities, chances, events, circumstances, and experiences from which to choose how to live these human lives. The choice is ours! We can take advantage of manifestations or not. If we miss an opportunity, the souls collaborating on it will simply manifest another chance in a different context or timeframe.

Important Takeaways from Chapter 9

- Source is the only consciousness. Various aspects of Source's vast mind work collaboratively to manifest what humans experience as physical matter and physical life. I call it co-creating, rather than just manifesting, only because it is easier to understand our role in the process if we think of it as two or more Light Beings collaborating. It is all really just one deity thinking.

- Our beliefs as eternal beings and as souls are manifested in the physical world.

- Every moment of human life is manifested by some part of Source, as are humans themselves. But life is not controlled by Source in the sense that Source intends specific outcomes.

- We Light Being souls manifest in concert with the parts of us still in the afterlife and with each other.

- We souls do not compete with each other when manifesting. Only our human bodies are competitive. We Light Beings within Source are collaborative.

10

Manifest Self-Healing

WE ARE POWERFUL ASPECTS OF OUR CREATOR INhabiting human bodies that Source (via its process of evolution) has designed to be self-healing. I learned in the afterlife that there is no reason why the combined body/Light Being soul entity cannot heal most illnesses and injuries. No reason why we have to continue to suffer physical and emotional pain beyond the normal healing period. Many physical and emotional wounds can be cured completely, without the intervention of anyone else, through manifesting. In addition, Knowings I received while in the Light showed me that Energy healing modalities such as Reiki and Healing Touch, along with some simple self-healing techniques, can work wonders for our bodies' health and our own well-being.

Because two entities are combined into one in these bodies, two separate healing abilities co-exist. The body has a manifested built-in ability to physically heal itself, regenerate tissue, and remove toxins. It also has the ability to discharge the pent-up energy that contributes to emotional problems. We Light Beings have our own innate ability to heal the body, and to resolve emotional traumas to ourselves and to our hosts that are caused by human life. Resolving trauma and emotional injuries is an innate part of our spiritual abilities as Source. We can change the character of any type of physical matter including, to some extent, our host bodies through reshaping Source's thought Energy. This is what Energy-based therapists help us do.

If you do not believe that you have powers beyond those of mortal men, you will never be able to heal yourself through conscious manifesting. Your belief will stand in your way because we Light Beings manifest into physical reality only what we truly and deeply believe in our heart of hearts. Maybe it will help to know that even scientists recognize and accept some forms of manifesting. One is called biofeedback. Using biofeedback you train your body to lower its heart rate, blood pressure, temperature, or pain level. All you do is use "attention" to that body part combined with the intention to lower the parameter you are focused on. The biofeedback machine shows you the positive results, which validates your efforts. Another form of manifesting that science accepts is what physicians call the placebo effect. In some clinical drug trials, the drug being tested works only a few percentage points better than the sugar pill because the patient getting the placebo believes he/she is getting the drug and heals through manifesting.

You must believe in manifested self-healing for it to work. That is because Energy-based healing depends upon "attention and intention," which is the manifesting formula. An outside therapist can provide some of the attention and intention to match yours to co-create healing. But you must join in that intention.

Afterlife Lessons On Self-Healing

Shortly after I entered the Light, a wealth of diverse Knowings entered my mind, explaining to me many of the things I was curious about while living forty-three years as Nanci. I received a huge download of knowledge about humans, including how they evolved. Knowings explained that all physical manifestations are Source-designed to evolve over time and that many are designed to self-repair. More Knowings showed me that Energy healing techniques work the best because they employ co-manifesting.

Some of the Knowings I received can most closely be translated into terms of how Source's thought Energy works. For lack of better terminology, I mentally translated concepts about humans and physical matter into terms of Source Energy signals, vibrations, frequencies, or tones—all terms I associate with energy. For example, I understand that healing depends upon body and soul working together to harmonize their Energies. I also translated most of the Knowings about humans and their healing abilities into scientific terms, probably because one of my college degrees is a Bachelor of Science in Biology, with a double major in vertebrate anatomy and physiology and chemistry. Since my afterlife visit, I have stumbled upon scientific explanations that appear to me to mean the same thing I learned in the Light. Sometimes the scientists even use energy terms.

I was given another download of Knowings specifically about how humans misunderstand what they call "mental illness." I was interested in this topic while I was earning a Bachelor of Arts degree in Psychology. I recall very little of these Knowings, only that some of the conditions medical science calls mental illness are really the display of a Light Being spiritual ability shining through the human's behavior. These abilities are outside the range of human behavior, so they are labeled abnormal and assumed to be defects or illnesses.

Most important, after merging with the rest of my Energy that had remained behind in heaven, I got a download about how we souls can use manifesting to heal.

Physical Self-Healing

Human bodies suffer different types of problems, only some of which we can heal to our satisfaction. Here is a list I was given in the afterlife of what will heal and what will not:

Congenital defects generally result from *in utero* DNA damage and will probably not be healed through the processes discussed below. There are obviously exceptions, however. As an example, I was born with a defective heart condition my cardiologist diagnosed as mitral valve prolapse with regurgitation. There were extra little flaps of skin on the edges of my heart's mitral valve that billowed out with every heartbeat when the valve opened to move blood through the heart. The result was that sometimes those flaps scooped up blood as they closed and propelled that blood backwards through the valve's opening. It was interesting to watch on color ultrasound but often painful to experience. When under stress, I fairly regularly had symptoms that felt to me like how I imagined a heart attack would feel. Before I started radiation therapy for metastatic breast cancer in 2011, I asked a friend who is a Reiki Master to do Energy healing on me while I was in the radiation chamber. She did it from her home every weekday for seven weeks. At the same time, I repeated over and over my intention to absorb only that amount of radiation needed to heal me and I sent the rest of the energy out to the people on my healing intentions list. One day my friend doing Reiki called me and told me the strangest thing had happened during one of her sessions while I was undergoing radiation. She said she saw what looked like scar tissue detaching from my heart and flying out of my body. Not long after that I started experiencing heart palpitations during radiation treatments and went to my cardiologist for help. He performed an echocardiogram of my heart and was shocked to see that my mitral valve prolapse was healed. The little flaps on the edges of the valve were gone! They are still gone to this day.

Physical injuries like broken bones and wounds can be healed, but there may be some residual disability that makes us unhappy. For example, if a leg is amputated, the surgical wounds will heal but the leg will not grow back. I learned in the afterlife that part of the reason humans cannot regrow limbs is because they do not believe they can. Consequently, we souls inside them do not believe we can regrow our hosts' limbs and we do not manifest that result. I keep telling my surgical oncologist that I am going to grow a new breast to replace the one he amputated. He just laughs. But I have already regained the sensation that it is there. I think I am afraid to actually regrow the breast's mass because my body fears it would be tumor instead of healthy tissue.

Acquired illnesses, like pneumonia and ulcers, can be healed completely.

Cellular dysfunction, like cancer, can be healed to a state medicine calls "remission" or "a personal cure."

The effects of living and aging, like skin thinning, muscle atrophy, hair loss, and loss of dexterity can be slowed down, but not eliminated. Every manifestation has a built-in life cycle because Source designed it that way. Humans suffer old age just like every other animal does. Even the universe itself has a life cycle. I was shown in the afterlife that our universe is in the "backswing" of its parabolic life cycle—in effect, old age. At some point all the Energy that Source expelled to manifest the universe will collapse upon itself in Source's mind and this universe will end.

Physical self-healing is a built-in biological ability. Source did not manifest the human animal as it presently appears. Rather, it manifested the *biological processes* that then generated humans through the Source-designed process of evolution. (Thus the age-old debate of divine design vs. evolution is moot. According to what I learned in the Light, both sides are right.) These processes include self-repair and homeostasis.

. Every cell of the body contains DNA sufficient to create an entire human body. The reason we do not have humans growing out of our ears and internal organs is because early in the development of a fetus (3 to 5 days) genes turn on and off in various cells that cause the cells to differentiate into specific functions. Some cells become liver cells and will never be anything else. Some cells become skin cells and remain so for life. Most differentiated cells do divide and reproduce themselves when called upon to do so to repair injury or cell damage. You see this in action when you cut yourself and new skin cells grow to repair the cut.

You may have heard of stem cells, defined as cells that retain the embryonic ability to remain undifferentiated and to turn into any type of tissue the body needs to repair itself. According to the NIH white paper titled "Stem Cell Basics I," before the differentiation process occurs in the tiny fetus, all cells have the ability to become any part of the body.[73] Scientists call cells in this state "stem cells." Some stem cells remain undifferentiated into specific types of body tissues even after the body is fully formed. These are the ones that can be recruited to transform into cells needed to repair damage. Each of our bodies has a store of embryonic stem cells.

Various parts of the body are constantly sloughing off and replacing old or damaged cells everywhere. According to my dermatologist, all of our skin is replaced over a cycle of about 27 to 30 days. The stomach lining grows anew about every five days. Cells located in these organs and tissues regularly divide and provide replacement cells. This maintenance cycle gives bodies the opportunity to heal.

The human body naturally seeks homeostasis—a state of balance. Human homeostasis refers to the body's ability to regulate physiologically its inner environment to ensure its stability in response to fluctuations in the outside environment. The liver, kidneys, brain, autonomic nervous system, and the endocrine system help maintain homeostasis. For example, the liver is responsible for metabolizing toxic substances and maintaining carbohydrate metabolism. The kidneys are responsible for regulating blood water levels, reabsorption of substances into the blood, maintenance of salt and ion levels in the blood, regulation of blood pH, and the excretion of wastes. When a stimulus triggers an imbalance, the body's self-regulatory processes go to work to restore balance. This is another healing power humans have.

Biological healing is automatic, unless you do something to prevent it. Cellular repair and homeostasis are automatic processess. But humans constantly prevent their own healing by their lifestyle choices. We souls have to convince our bodies to stop doing the things that make them sick. Examples are: a job that is too stressful, smoking, overeating, eating the wrong foods, drinking alcohol, using recreational drugs, failing to get exercise, toxic relationships, refusing to set boundaries for others who abuse us, unsafe sex, overexerting ourselves when we are out of shape, allowing our children to run our lives, living too fast a lifestyle, repressing emotions, and more. We have to overcome human denial of the effects of these choices. Do not be like the man who jumps off a 50-story building and all the way down says to himself: "So far so good, so far so good." Or the man whose family says: "But he was never sick a day in his life!"—after he dies of a heart attack.

Take care of problems right away and completely or they may get integrated into your cellular and "soulular" memory and get reproduced long-term. Remember: we manifest what we truly and deeply believe. If we believe we are ill or injured, that belief can be manifested into our lives beyond the normal healing period.

Physical Self-Healing Plan

The following self-healing plan for physical injuries and illnesses was outlined for me as part of the download of Knowings I received about manifesting. But I had to find the tools and techniques myself through experimentation. My suggested tools work for me, but you may have to experiment with them and others you find in order to identify the techniques that work best for you.

Step 1. Attention. You have to listen to your body. Really listen. It might help to sit down and actually do a periodic inventory of how each part of your host body is feeling. Touch your feet, rub each muscle, bend the toes, flex the ankle. Identify where you have pain. Then rub your calves. Go inch by inch from the ankle up and dig in to see if anything is sore. Especially check the tendons and muscle attachments. Continue going up the body all the way to your scalp, moving each part through its full range of motion. You might be amazed to find out how many sore spots you have been ignoring. Each pain tells a story about how you have been mistreating your body.

Step 2. Intention. You have to honestly intend to heal.

As an attorney who at one time defended medical malpractice

cases, I became familiar with the phenomenon that some people actually do not want to heal. There can be several different reasons, including the fact that humans have a tendency to become stuck, or form a habit, or get used to life being a certain way, and do not want to change simply because of the innate human resistance to change. Some people are afraid to heal because they are afraid of how it will change their daily lives. If they have been in a wheelchair for years, and suddenly they can walk, that changes everything in their daily routine and creates immediate fears about what the future now holds. It also may remove the barrier that allowed them to get out of working for a living.

Others identify with their illness or injury and think that if they heal they will be a different person and they cannot imagine what that person would be like. For example, someone who has been depressed for years and rarely goes out of the house will resist being happy because she does not remember how good it feels to live without depression. She cannot imagine what she will do with the time she used to spend feeling depressed, crying, sleeping, hiding away from people, and reading books or watching TV.

What attorneys call "secondary gain" may be at work. The ill or injured person has gotten a lot of attention and sympathy because of the condition and does not want to give that up by healing.

Step 3. Plan the work and work the plan. Healing is hard work and requires using common sense in your daily activities. The following is good advice that you have heard many times before and have ignored. Then you wonder why you have not healed. Healing takes time, dedication, and constant monitoring. There is a reason why nurses in hospitals take vital signs every few hours. You will need to monitor your own healing progress in order to recognize that it is happening.

I am not a physician and am not trying to diagnose or treat any medical or emotional condition. I merely offer you the information I was given in the afterlife, along with tools and techniques my own experiences have shown to work.

Sleep. We readily accept that our pets need a lot of sleep and accommodate them. But we are far less generous with the animals nearest and dearest to us—our bodies. "It's my body," we say, "and I can do whatever I want with it." While that may be true practically, it is not true spiritually or factually. Our bodies are also animals—animals that have been extremely giving, open, unconditionally loving, and willing to carry us souls around for decades. They do not *belong* to us any more than we souls belong to them. The same way that our pets are entrusted to us and create an obligation to care for them and meet their basic needs, our host bodies are entrusted to us at their birth with the understanding that we souls will take care of them the best we can. Sleep is a basic need of human animals and cannot be ignored or shortchanged.

The body's repair work is done primarily while it is asleep. So an adult must get seven to nine hours of uninterrupted sleep, especially while healing. If your husband snores, move into another bedroom during your healing phase. If you get up several times a night to use the bathroom, stop eating and drinking after 8 p.m. and/or consult your physician. If pain keeps you from sleeping, use a device to find a better position (like a sleeping wedge or pillow), get a new bed (like a Sleep Number bed that takes pressure off your joints), or take pain relievers until you have healed.

Eat. Every parent puts a newborn on a strict feeding schedule because the baby is growing rapidly and needs constant nutrition to fuel cell reproduction. As adults, when we are in a healing phase we also grow new cells rapidly. Those cells need fuel on a structured routine basis just like babies do. So eat on schedule instead of grazing or skipping meals. And consume the foods and drinks that clinical trials have shown to promote healing for your medical condition.

Drink water. The bodies we inhabit consist mostly of water. Water is used to carry all the nutrients to the cells and to carry pollutants away from them. So drink enough water to keep your body well hydrated.

Exercise. Blood flow is what carries the nutrition to the cells that are working hard to divide and repair tissue damage. Exercise increases blood flow. It also keeps joints moving smoothly.

Lymphatic system self-massage. Doing manual lymph drainage is important for anyone who has lymphedema or an injury that causes swelling. The lymphatic system carries away the excess materials of cellular growth, as well as damaged cells, foreign bodies, drug residues, bacteria, and toxins and deposits them in the bloodstream to be filtered out by the kidneys. The reason deep breathing is so cleansing is because it removes cellular waste products by pumping lymph through the chest and emptying it into the bloodstream. Twice a day lymph system self-massage will help clear the lymph faster. A lymphedema therapist can show you the technique.

Pain reduction. *The Trigger Point Therapy Workbook* by Clair and Amber Davies is an excellent resource for identifying sources of pain and relieving it.[74] A trigger point is a small contraction knot in a muscle. You can feel it with your fingers if you dig for it. Trigger points may or may not be painful where they are located but they can cause radiated pain into areas that you do not attribute to the knot. That is where *The Trigger Point Therapy Workbook* comes in handy. It will tell you where to look for the trigger point by giving you diagrams of where you will feel the referred pain. I have found that the smaller the trigger point the more painful it is and the more referred pain it causes. Working out these trigger points can alleviate an incredible array of painful conditions that you or your physician have been attributing to something else.

You have to be willing to experience pain in order to heal it. Some healing is instant and painless. Some is not. The pain of old injuries may resurface in what is called "retracing" until the stored energy of the trauma that caused them is released. You have to be willing to suffer the side effects of energy rechanneling through your body, and of emotions coming to the surface and expressing themselves, if you want to heal. It may feel like your whole body is being rewired.

You may also feel a little sick when toxins once stored in tissues are released. In short, you have to suffer a little to heal and stick with it until you get the results you manifest.

Use drugs, exercise, electronic stimulation, muscle massage, and whatever else it takes to reduce or eliminate pain. Pain will color your attitude about life in general and create hindering beliefs that will affect your whole life if left untreated.

Reduce exposure to infection. Do not unnecessarily spend time in large crowds, around children, in gyms, or in public places. Use hand sanitizer constantly when exposed to others and when using grocery carts or touching other public surfaces. Sanitize your home and especially the things you touch frequently. This includes toilet seats and flush handles, phones, light switches, keyboards and keypads, and remote controls.

Use Energy-based healing modalities. Craniosacral therapy, Reiki, Network Chiropractic, Pranic Healing, Healing Touch, Focusing, and others are therapies that work with the energy of the body, removing blockages, and increasing integration of energy flow. I was informed in the afterlife that Energy modalities are the best way to heal our host bodies. I have read various human theories of what this Energy is, what it should be called (such as *chi*), and how it can be manipulated. I think all we need to know is that humans are created solely of Source's thought Energy and that Energy can be manifested and/or changed in any conceivable way.

Manifested Healing

In general, we manifest healing within the confines of the biological principles Source designed for the universe. For example, a person who weighs 500 pounds will not be able to use pure manifesting to reduce his weight to 175. He will have to radically alter his eating habits and exercise hard and often to lose the weight because that is how the biology of human animals works. Although it is possible for Source to manifest a svelte human body overnight, the results would most likely be taken by humans as a symptom of a life-threatening disease rather than as a spiritual phenomenon. So we Light Being souls, working with the rest of our Energy in the afterlife and following the laws of nature, tend to manifest healing in a way that is both believable to our hosts and acceptable to the culture in which we live.

Manifested Healing Plan

Step 1. Attention. Attention can take any form you choose. One method that worked for me is *The Healing Code*, which is a technique designed to help change hidden or unconscious beliefs that lead to physical or emotional problems.[75] The technique combines physical attention to doing the prescribed movements with specific intentions to heal. In my opinion, it is a useful tool for manifesting healing, though the technique itself has no physical healing power. For decades, the author, Alexander Loyd, PhD, ND, had been seeking a way to heal his wife's depression, even going so far as to leave the ministry and get a PhD in psychology and a doctorate in naturopathic medicine. Dr. Loyd says *The Healing Code* was mentally downloaded to him one day while he was on an airplane. He documented everything he could remember and created the *Healing Code* program he now sells.

The theory of *The Healing Code* is that every disease and disability has stress at its root—not emotional stress or anxiety, but physiological stress caused by the body being in a never-ending series of fight-or-flight responses. Dr. Candace Pert, formerly of the National Institutes of Mental Health, proved through her research that memories are stored everywhere in the body at the cellular level and that cells can become locked into unhealthy physical responses due to these memories of stress or trauma.[76] *The Healing Code* technique in theory uses the body's own energy and redirects it back into four neurological centers to provide a corrective or canceling energy to the energy stuck in cells. That, in turn, heals the memory at the cellular level and allows the locked-down cells to once again engage in repairs, according to Dr. Loyd.

Step 2. Intention. In 2011, for the two weeks between being diagnosed with metastatic breast cancer and the first round of surgeries, I tried *The Healing Code* technique to try to manifest a complete cure. I focused my attention on healing and spoke the following intention out loud several times a day:

> Nanci's Healing Code. It is my intention that all known and unknown negative images, all destructive cellular memories, and all damaging beliefs that relate in any way to my cancer diagnosis be healed, cured, and removed from the manifestation of the physical life of Nanci through my unconditional love and power as Source.

I meditated primarily with the general intention to heal. But sometimes I wanted the tumor simply to be gone when I got to the hospital, so that my body and I would not have to suffer all that follows an advanced cancer diagnosis.

On the day of surgery, moments after the hospital ultrasonographer put the wand on me to locate the tumor, I said to her: "You're going to tell me that you can't find the tumor, aren't you?" "How'd you know that?" she asked. I responded: "Because I disappeared it. I healed it." She asked me how. "With healing energy," I responded. I explained to her that dear friends who are energy healers had done Reiki and Healing Touch on me, that I had been doing *The Healing Code*, and that thousands of people all over the world were praying for me, intending my healing. The ultrasound tech told me that this situation had occurred only once before, and that the other woman had said the same thing: that she had used energy healing to cure herself. I asked what they had done in that other patient's case. She told me that the woman had been sent home and was told to come back in six months, while the hospital staff all hoped for the best. She said I would probably be sent home too. *Voila! I did it!,* I thought.

After an hour of the ultrasonographer and radiologist together trying to locate the tumor by comparing their images with those taken at the time of biopsy, the radiologist gave up. I started doing the happy dance (to the extent I could while lying on my side on a table), thinking I was going home. But the radiologist had called my surgical oncologist, who told her to send me over to the outpatient breast center to see if the ultrasonographer who found the tumor for biopsy could find it again with her digital equipment. So my friend drove me to the breast center, the same ultrasonographer was called in from home to do the imaging, and she did indeed find the tumor. A radiologist at the breast center then stuck a wire into the tumor to mark it, bandaged me up and wrapped my chest in plastic, and sent me back to the hospital for surgery.

The moral of the story: When you frame your manifesting intentions, think through what you really want. It was not a good idea for me to specifically intend that the tumor be gone when my caregivers went looking for it. I should have intended generally a full and immediate cure from the cancer. Manifesting the tumor's disappearance on ultrasound could have indicated a cure, but, it could also have meant an erroneous ultrasound reading and delayed treatment while the tumor grew. I had not thought of this possibility when framing my intentions. During the month between finding the primary tumor and positive lymph node during the first surgery, and the second surgery for a radical mastectomy and axillary lymph node removal, cancer cells had taken over my entire breast, all the way down to the chest wall, along with several more axillary lymph nodes, making me a Stage 3 cancer patient. If my surgical oncologist had not insisted on repeating the ultrasound with the newer digital equipment at the outpatient breast center, I would probably not be alive today.

Step 3. Plan the work and work the plan. Your manifesting healing plan will depend upon the type of issue you are trying to heal.

Pain. Source intended pain to be a signal that something is biologically wrong. It is not meant to be a constant companion. So you do not have to accept constant pain as a punishment, or God's will, or what you deserve, or for any other human logic reason.

Co-manifesting and love can help reduce pain, as it did for me during my 2011 breast biopsies. When my mammogram was interpreted as suspicious for a tumor in early May 2011, my surgical oncologist scheduled me for a biopsy. The procedure was going to be tricky because I am allergic to a lot of drugs and medical supplies and have bad reactions to pain killers. So I recruited the help of the Energy healers I know around the world, and my readers, to send me healing energy to help get me through the procedure without any medication. The radiologist who did the procedure told me he was very nervous because he had never done needle biopsies on a breast cancer patient without anesthetic, and he had to push the needle in very deep three times to get the specimen tissue. One of the nurses decided to rub my legs during the procedure because there is clinical evidence that sending the brain confusing sensory signals helps reduce pain. The other nurse held my hand to help give me strength. The procedure went just fine. At the end, the radiologist exclaimed, "I've never felt so much love in a room before! What was going on here?" I told him that my readers and spiritual healers had been sending me love and healing intentions to get me through the biopsies without anesthesia or pain killers. I knew I felt it, but I was surprised that the radiologist felt it too!

In addition to traditional methods of pain control, try bringing your attention to the pain and intend for it to dissipate.

> *Nanci's crystal meditation*. Assume a comfortable position. Close your eyes. Relax and center yourself. Hold an eight-sided crystal in your hand. Bring your attention to the pain in your body. Focus on it but do not suffer from it. Maintain an objective perspective. Look deeply into the crystal. Now in your mind, shrink yourself down smaller and smaller so that the crystal appears to be a multi-story building or skyscraper. Walk around the outside of the crystal, noticing its smooth clear surface and facets. Eventually you discover a secret door in one side of the crystal,

> the outline of which can only be seen from one angle. Open the door and step into the crystal. Go to the center and look up. Far up in the tiptop of the crystal you can see light. The light shines directly on you. Expand the light so that it totally surrounds you. Bathe in it. Breathe it in, over and over. Let the light fill your senses. Let it fill your whole being. Open your body and mind to the light. Pull it into your arms and legs all the way down to your fingers and toes. When you feel like you are bursting with light, drop your pain on the floor of the crystal and step away from it. Watch the light burn up the pain until it disappears in a puff of steam. Then turn around and walk back to the door in the crystal and step out. Come back to full size and open your eyes. Know that you left the pain in the crystal.[77]

Side effects from drugs or therapies like radiation. While you are taking the drug or treatment, form the intention that you will accept only so much of it as is necessary to heal your condition and that you intend to convert the rest to healing Energy to send out to others. Tell your body to flush out of its tissues the parts of the drug or treatment that are not directly contributing to your wellness.

Diabetes, cancer, damage to DNA. Use Nanci's Healing Code after examining the behaviors and beliefs that gave rise to the condition. For example, the primary cause of diabetes is unhealthy eating. The core belief behind overeating might be, "It will make me feel better," "I can fill up the hole in my heart with food," "Food will not reject me," "This little bit won't hurt," "I'll make up for it by working out later," etc. Manifesting follows beliefs. You will continue to manifest a need to overeat as long as you continue to believe whatever it is that allows you to justify the behavior. Use Nanci's Healing Code, for example, to manifest healing of the old belief and then *train* your body to a new belief (see below).

Cancer and other DNA-damaged diseases can be healed by repairing DNA, which is a normal bodily function that has been disrupted by physiological stress. Use Nanci's Healing Code.

Surgery. As you are going into surgery, form the intention that the procedure will go well and that you will heal quickly from it. If you try to form specific result-oriented intentions, such as, "I won't die on the table" or "I won't have any disability as a result of the surgery," you might end up with the result you want but miss out on a better result that might have been yours if you had used a more general intention instead of a narrow one. For example, you might miss an NDE that would have brought you peace and freedom from a fear of death and a full cure! Or you might miss out on a temporary disability that required physical therapy paid for by insurance and which ended up healing another problem that insurance would not pay for.

Manifest a new reality around a chronic condition. I have heard people say, "I feel the way I feel. I can't change that." We *can* change our attitude about an illness or physical condition, which will change how your body feels. You know this. You have done it a million times in your life, especially if you are a parent who has had to function despite great pain or illness. You have cheered yourself up using all kinds of different tricks. You can do the same thing with physical ailments by consciously choosing a better attitude. Is it easy? Of course not. Is it fun? No. But the results are a whole lot better than believing that you are doomed to suffer. You may just need to change your focus from the emotion or physical condition to something that lifts you up or pleases you. Music, sunshine, friends, and loved ones can help with this.

How do you do it? Jack, the surgeon stranded on an island on the former TV show *Lost,* had a great way of humanizing the formula. He said, "When I get scared in a surgery I let my emotions run wild for ten seconds. Then I say, 'Enough,' and pull myself together and do my job." That is exactly what you should do. You honor what your body is feeling for a short while—how long a while will depend upon what you are feeling. But then you take control over your own life and tell your body "that's enough." Say: "You've been depressed long enough." "You've been angry/resentful/whatever long enough." "You've been in pain long enough. I'm not spending any more of my precious time on earth mired in that painful place." And then work on finding a different way to look at your situation. You may need help getting to that better attitude, such as by using Mindfulness. A good therapist or insightful friend who will listen objectively to you can also help by giving you a different perspective.

In 2005, I was in an automobile accident that resulted in traumatic scoliosis (abnormal curvature) of my spine in the neck and upper back. The radiologist who read my first x-rays misdiagnosed it as congenital scoliosis, a birth defect. When the pain kept getting worse, and I could not sit back in a chair or lie on my back, I referred myself to a physical medicine specialist. He thought the pain could be resolved by physical therapy. After a couple of weeks the physical therapy resulted in three bulging discs in my neck, and the therapist referred me to a neurologist. The neurologist correctly diagnosed and treated my condition seven months after the accident. The scoliosis resolved, but left weakness in the muscles holding my spine in place such that I have the chronic problem of my back "going out" on occasion. I still have the disc herniations and some neck pain. As you might imagine, I was a little angry about the teenager whose car hit my car broadside and about the repeated misdiagnoses. I could not get over that anger on my own, so I went to a practitioner who specializes in Focusing and somatic trauma resolution. She explained to me that, because of a preexisting neck injury from the 1980s, if my spine had not deformed the way it did to dissipate the impact, my neck probably would have snapped and I would be paralyzed from the neck down. That simple statement completely dissolved my anger. It gave me a new perspective on the injuries. I went from anger to gratitude that my spine had sacrificed itself to prevent worse injury. I love my body for how she took care of us both to the best of her ability under very dangerous conditions.

Train your body. We have all heard the saying, "trust your gut." That may or may not be good advice depending upon what your gut is accustomed to feeling. If you have accumulated a lot of untrue beliefs, your gut will tell you to take an action informed by those false beliefs. How many times have you seen people do something to get revenge when they have been hurt and then suffer the consequences of their revenge? Or escalate a fight when it would have been smarter to calm things down? We always act according to what we believe. So people who act this way believe it makes sense. But what it really represents is animal instinct—violence, competitiveness, territorialism. That animal gut instinct will get you into trouble every single time. You have to *train* your gut to more rational and effective reactions before you can trust it to guide you in the future.

In *BACKWARDS: Returning to Our Source for Answers*, I outlined the following self-training tool I created to help change my own bad habit formed from a childhood belief that witty snide remarks, like what a standup comedian says, are funny:

> I once had a terrible habit of saying anything that popped into my head, including some very unkind and hurtful things. Some were disguised in the form of humor, but were still biting. After my beyond-death experience I tried harder to break this habit.
>
> I started by paying more attention to what I was saying. I *listened* to myself. At first I did not *hear* what I said, or at least realize its hurtful content, until days or weeks after the fact. I resolved to try to be more aware of how my comments affected others. Eventually I started realizing something I said was hurtful within days of saying it, instead of weeks. Then, with renewed attention and intention, I shortened the time lag to hours instead of days. Finally, with perseverance, I was able to recognize my insults right after they flew out of my mouth.
>
> Hearing some of what I said made me ashamed

> of myself. So I apologized sincerely to the person to whom I said it. At first that apology came weeks after the fact, then days, then hours, then immediately after I made the hurtful remark, as I built up the courage to confess my hurtful behavior and take responsibility for it.
>
> I reasoned that, now that I was "catching" my bad habit right after I engaged in it, I should be able to catch those nasty words before I said them. At first I did not notice an insult was escaping until near the end. Then over time I would catch them half way through. Finally, after months and months of practice, I recognized an insult in formation before it flew through my teeth and I was able to bite down on it.
>
> I resolved next to catch the snide remarks as they were forming in my mind. At first they seemed to just *be* there instantly. All I could do was just keep them there in my mind but not let them out of my mouth. For years I walked around with a continuous monologue of wisecracks, snide remarks, and snippy comments going on in my head at the same time I was trying to carry on a respectful conversation. Many times I had to apologize to someone for laughing inappropriately or having a look on my face completely out of line with what they were saying, explaining that I was reacting to the laugh track in my head, and not what they were telling me. Eventually the hurtful thoughts stopped.[78]

It will take self-discipline to use this tool until it becomes a habit. But it will not be the human's self-discipline. It will be *yours* and you are a powerful part of Source capable of creating reality. You can *do this*. Then you can start manifesting from within a healthier belief framework.

Emotional Self-Healing

Know the difference between a physical ailment and an emotional one. I learned in the afterlife that illness results from damage to the functioning of the biological and chemical processes that Source designed into humans. We get a cut and it gets infected. We have contact with a bacterium or virus and get sick. We fall and break a limb. Our genes misfire or degrade or mutate and then some body system no longer works as intended. We overeat, overindulge in drinking, or overuse medications, and we damage our bodies. All these illnesses and injuries are predictable because they follow the known paths discovered through science. They are also generally curable, either by allowing them to run their course and be healed via our immune systems or through the intervention of medical science, Energy healing, and manifesting.

Some therapists and spiritual authors blame every ache and pain on emotions. I learned that breaking a leg is a physical and mechanical disturbance to the biological processes, not an Energy imbalance or emotional problem made manifest. An emotional problem may have contributed to the events giving rise to the leg breaking, such as self-destructive risk-taking behavior, but the immediate cause of the break is a disruption in the continuity of bone. That break will heal itself over time. But if you want it to heal straight, and not get infected, medical intervention is needed. So the healing plan should include getting an x-ray and fixation of the break.

Similarly, infections are caused by bacteria or viruses, not Energy imbalances or emotional problems. The body will likely fight off a minor infection if you get plenty of rest and allow the immune system to work. More complicated infectious agents will require the intervention of drugs designed to kill them or make their habitat inhospitable. Again, the healing plan should include a trip to the doctor and a prescription.

It is possible that our human's thinking can make us sick, but only if we truly and deeply believe that those illness-producing thoughts constitute our current reality. The most prevalent form of this phenomenon is the continuation of an illness or injury long after it should have healed. For reasons we cannot consciously fathom, we come to believe that the illness or injury *is* us. The human victim mentality convinces us that we are asthmatic, or anxious, or depressed, or handicapped, and we incorporate this condition into our beliefs about ourselves for the rest of our lives. Practically speaking, there is no reason why, for example, a skin condition should continue to exist after all the skin cells that once had that condition have been replaced through the body's normal healing and regeneration processes. Nor is there a good reason why depression should continue after a course of antidepressants has corrected the chemical imbalance in the brain. Yet both conditions do sometimes persist. These and other conditions are ripe for manifested healing.

Emotional problems can turn into ailments. In her groundbreaking book, *Molecules of Emotion: The Science Behind Mind-Body Medicine*, Candace B. Pert, PhD, who was then a Research Professor in the Department of Physiology and Biophysics at Georgetown University School of Medicine, explains the biophysics of how emotional traumas become trapped in bodies at the site of the injury. Attached to each cell, floating on its oily outer membrane, are molecules called "receptors" made up of proteins. Dr. Pert tells us that receptor cells act like sensing molecules or scanners picking up messages carried by various peptides.[79] The messages are delivered when peptides bump into and stick for a second to the scanning receptor molecule until information enters the cell. The message might be to manufacture new proteins, begin cellular division, or another biological task.

Dr. Pert says that all sensory information goes through a filtering process as it travels across nerve synapses, getting associated with events or stimuli occurring at the same time. Only a small portion of these events or stimuli make it into our conscious attention. Peptides attaching to receptors on cells determine what gets through the filtering process, thereby selecting what we pay attention to from moment to moment. "Using neuropeptides as the cue, our bodymind retrieves or represses emotions and behaviors," Dr. Pert writes.[80] In Dr. Pert's research, she uses the term "emotions" to include anger, fear, sadness, joy, and contentment; pleasure and pain; the physical drives of hunger, thirst, and sexual attraction; and subjective experiences such as inspiration, awe, bliss, and other states of consciousness.

Memories are stored all over the body by the actions of peptides on receptors. Dr. Pert adds: "Repressed traumas caused by overwhelming emotion can be stored in a body part, thereafter affecting our ability to feel that part or even move it. … Trauma and blockage of emotional and physical information can be stored indefinitely at the cellular level."[81] Repressing emotions causes a major disruption in the flow of peptides and the information they distribute. Cells rely upon getting feedback from other cells to know whether to keep pouring out a particular peptide. When peptide movement is inhibited, it affects all the autonomic processes regulated by peptides, like breathing, blood flow, immunity, digestion, and elimination, which then collapse down to a few simple feedback loops and upset the normal healing response. These feedback loops have to be broken for healing to begin.

One way to reverse the feedback loop is by consciously doing something that causes the peptides to alter their behavior, such as holding your breath, breathing faster, or releasing a burst of anger, all of which Dr. Pert says cause the rapid release of peptides in an effort to restore homeostasis. Meditation, along with allowing long-buried thoughts and feelings to surface, is a way of getting the peptides flowing again, returning the body and emotions to health. You can use meditation to focus your attention and intention on healing a specific area. Dr. Pert tells the story in her book of an athlete whose doctor told him elbow injuries take a long time to heal because the elbow gets so little blood flow. The athlete meditated every day for 20 minutes on increasing blood flow to his injured elbow and healed it very quickly.

I achieved a similar result using Dr. Eugene Gendlin's Focusing technique. For a while after an auto accident, my legs felt freezing cold. I tried heating pads, leg warmers, blankets, and warmer clothing (in the summer) but nothing would warm them up. So I went to a certified Focusing practitioner, who asked me questions to elicit the cause of the coldness. Believe it or not, the answer my body gave me was that my legs felt responsible for the accident because they froze and did not accelerate away from the oncoming car fast enough to avoid the collision. They had stayed in the freeze part of the fight-flight-freeze response to trauma since the accident. I thought the whole thing was kind of crazy. But once we identified that erroneous belief, and acknowledged that it was not my legs' fault that I was injured and that they were not literally frozen, my legs warmed right up and stayed that way.

Emotional Self-Healing Plan

You have buried strong emotions deep inside yourself, maybe the strongest of your life! It is going to hurt when they come up—physically, and emotionally. But experts in trauma resolution agree that you do *not* have to remember and relive the memories of all the stored traumas in order to release them. All you have to do is release their trapped energy.

Step 1. Attention. Be on the lookout for increased activity or symptoms that could tell you an emotional problem is hiding inside. For example, when I subconsciously feel that some new insight or memory is bubbling up and about to come to the surface, I eat everything in sight. Sometimes when we eat, especially if we are not really hungry, we are using food to help push down into unawareness emotions or insights we have been avoiding. The more we have to hide from ourselves, the more we eat. So pay attention if your eating picks up suddenly. Ask yourself: "How am I feeling right now?" Eating does not have to be your mechanism. It could be exercising, shopping, sexual activity, drinking, working, etc.—whatever you typically use to escape your feelings.

Step 2. Intention. Resolve to change your perspective on the symptom or condition. Consider the example of my crooked spine and how my Focusing practitioner's comment changed my whole perspective on it and helped it heal.

Find something to love about the situation giving you emotional problems. In 2001, almost exactly seven years after my major NDE,[82] I suddenly became very ill. My body temperature often dropped down to 95 degrees, my blood pressure and heart rate fluctuated wildly on an hourly basis, and I could not physically sit upright for long periods of time. My family physician and cardiologist were stumped. They did their best to treat the symptoms, but had no treatment plan for me. Apparently I had one of my own: I began waking up at 4:30 am with my mind full of memories of what I experienced and learned in the afterlife. I wrote it all down and soon realized my writings constituted a book manuscript, complete with a table of contents and title. I spent most of that year writing because I was too ill to work as an attorney. The result was a 700-page manuscript that I divided into my first and second *BACKWARDS* books. It took at least a year for my body to start to recover from whatever was wrong with it, but it slowly did. And, though I hated the loss of a year's worth of income, and the terror of never knowing whether my vital signs would be stable for any length of time, I loved writing the books.

Ask for co-creators to help. You can enlist the assistance of other Light Beings to help you manifest healing, not to manifest for you but to add their healing Energy and intentions to your own. My request for assistance from other Light Beings who love me is: "If it is consistent with my goals for being here, I ask all other Light Beings within Source who love me to add healing intentions to my own and send me Energy to help me heal myself and manifest wellness."

Step 3. Plan the work and work the plan. Some of the emotional self-healing tools I have used successfully are:

Focusing. Focusing, a process developed by Eugene Gendlin, PhD, is a good self-help technique to use when you have pain or discomfort but do not know what is causing it. The process is described in brief in Chapter 6, Step 2, and in full in the book *Focusing.*[83]

Somatic Experiencing; Somatic Trauma Resolution. This self-help technique releases the stuck energy of physical and emotional traumas from injuries, resolving the wide array of medical conditions those traumas generate. The science behind the technique is described in detail in *Waking the Tiger: Healing Trauma* by Peter A. Levine, who holds a PhD in Medical and Biological Physics from UC Berkeley.[84]

Diane Poole Heller, PhD, and Laurence S. Heller, PhD, authors of *Crash Course: A Self-Healing Guide to Auto Accident Trauma & Recovery*, state that the reptilian part of our brains, the hindbrain, controls the flight-fight-freeze response to danger or attack just as it does in jungle animals.[85] Animals in the wild whose flight-fight-freeze response is activated physically shake it off after the danger passes. They tremble and flinch until all the energy triggered by adrenaline and cortisol is released. But, in human society, the flight-fight-freeze response is triggered too often—by things that are not true dangers, such as stressful job or family expectations—and we are trained not to react to the powerful hormones circulating in our bodies. How many times have you seen a corporate executive shake, tremble, and twitch after completing a stressful project? No one has. All that emotional energy gets stored in the body and trapped without a release. It then creates the trauma feedback loops Dr. Pert discusses in *Molecules of Emotion*.

An important aspect of somatic trauma release is to resist repeatedly telling the story of how you were injured: "When you tell the story [of your trauma] your body is also listening and begins to respond to the sense of danger again and again. Repetition of the accident story can actually intensify the trauma, which overactivates the nervous system again," writes Dr. Heller.[86]

The Presence Process. This self-help technique works to resolve repetitive emotional traumas, like picking the same wrong type friend or lover over and over, or getting into the same argument over the same issues over and over. It is a meditation program in ten steps (10 weeks) that very gently leads you into your past to recognize the recurring patterns of trauma and where they started.

The first step of *The Presence Process* teaches you a breathing method that helps release the peptide endorphin.[87] The second step teaches you that other people who cause conflict and strong emotions are doing you the favor of being a messenger to get you to see what it is you have been hiding from yourself—usually a suppressed memory that you are projecting onto another person. Step 3 asks you to identify the patterns of behavior you have adopted from someone else (usually your parents) to deal with this particular emotional upset. Steps 4 and 5 focus your attention on unresolved childhood emotions, asking you to cry them out and reassure your inner child that the trauma is over and that you have more tools as an adult to deal with upsets. Step 6 teaches an emotional cleansing process. Step 7 teaches how to be physically present and aware of bodily sensations. Step 8 focuses on self-forgiveness and forgiveness of others. Step 9 asks you to directly focus on how your intimate relationships have ended by filling in the blanks in the following phrases: "We also end up," or "I always end up … and they always end up." You then follow this pattern back in time to see where it started and with whom. Step 10 asks you to accept yourself as you are—a perfect reflection of the One who made you.

Mindfulness. Mindfulness is best described by Jon Kabat-Zinn, PhD, in *Full Catastrophe Living*.[88] While a Professor of Medicine at the University of Massachusetts Medical School, Dr. Kabat-Zinn created Mindfulness as a clinically validated program for UMass's Stress Reduction Clinic. Dr. Kabat-Zinn earned his PhD in molecular biology from MIT in 1971 in the laboratory of Nobel Laureate Salvador Luria and therefore brings science to this meditative healing process. In essence, mindfulness is the meditative practice of paying attention on purpose, in the present moment, without judging any thought that enters your mind. It helps you become more aware of your body, your thoughts, and your attitudes, and provides a process by which you can use that new awareness to reduce the stress and pain of long term illness and trauma.

Important Takeaways from Chapter 10

- Your body has innate healing abilities. You have innate spiritual healing powers. Together, you and your body have all the tools you need to heal most of life's pains and illnesses.
- While miracles are possible with manifesting, we Light Beings generally work within the parameters of healing that our host bodies and their cultures are accustomed to accepting.
- The most effective healing occurs when you take the time to get to the root cause of the condition bothering you and resolve it at its physical or emotional source.
- You can manifest self-healing through attention, intention, and working the healing plans outlined above.
- If a particular condition cannot be fully healed, you can manifest a way to accept and live with the chronic condition with less pain and trauma, using the tools outlined above.

11

Troubleshooting

WHEN PEOPLE SAY THEY HAVE TRIED CONSCIOUS manifesting but it did not work for them, what do they mean? Manifesting always works—every single second of your life. You are constantly manifesting everything around you. Everything you see, hear, smell, perceive is manifested by Source in the form of you, the souls around you, and All Those With An Interest In Earth, all parts of the divine entity Source. My readers often tell me they tried to manifest a new home, job, love interest, or something else and it did not work. They ask how that could happen when I had just told them that manifesting always works.

There are a number of reasons why you do not see what you expect to see as the result of conscious manifesting. The following are a few problems that may be holding you up.

You cannot focus on manifesting. The best tool for conscious manifesting is meditation. Try thinking of meditation as concentration rather than as an unobtainable mystical state of mind. Use the same type and level of concentration you use to prepare your tax return, pick teams for fantasy football, balance your checkbook, search the Internet, or track down your lost keys. Instead of focusing on taxes or keys, focus on nothing. Try looking at a blank wall and concentrating on what you see there. That type of mental state is all you need. While you are in that mental state, give your attention to what you want to manifest and set your intention to will the subject of your attention into existence.

If you have trouble concentrating, try the exercises at the end of each chapter in *The Master Key System.* Charles Haanel designed them specifically to teach his students how to focus their minds.

There is a time delay between efforts and results. Often there is a time delay between our "attention and intention" and results because of the linear aspect of the human experience. This does not mean you are not consciously manifesting. It might mean you are not *aware* of what you consciously manifested because your human is looking for something specific and that is not what you created.

The difference between manifesting when you are in the afterlife versus when you are in the body is that conscious manifesting is not instantaneous here. Every once in a while it will be, but not often enough for most of us. You may sometimes say: "Oh, I'd really like to talk to Sally," and a few minutes later she calls. So some conscious intentions do instantaneously manifest while we are in the body. Some manifestations will appear very quickly while others seem to take months or years.

All I can say is keep your eyes, ears, and heart open, and stay in the present moment, so you can *recognize* your manifestation when it appears.

Your manifestations take a different form than expected. For example, I consciously manifested an improvement in my immune system. I thought I would magically feel better. What I got was a blood test result showing a Vitamin D deficiency. That sure did not seem like what I intended to manifest. But it was! Taking the Vitamin D supplement boosted my immune system. So, sometimes our manifestation presents in the form of a problem whose solution turns out to be exactly what we wanted.

Most of our manifestations take the form of an experience, event, situation, or opportunity. Look for anything you might call a coincidence or ironic, or perhaps you would call it a sign or omen. Those are your manifestations.

You give up too soon. This is a common problem. We all need reinforcement and reassurance that our chosen plan of action actually works. But I find the best success story is one's own; success breeds success. You have to practice consciously manifesting the same way your body practiced learning how to walk, feed itself, ride a bike, etc. Start with something small. For instance, put your attention on having something good to eat today. Expect the tasty food to appear. Then see what happens. Maybe someone will invite you to lunch out of the blue. Or you find something good in your refrigerator that you forgot you bought. Or you spontaneously get a craving for something good to eat that you have to go out to buy. You manifested the opportunity to eat the good food, not the food itself. If this exercise produces the desired result, try another small manifestation, like putting your attention on finding a lost item and intending to find it. Keep building small successes like that and work your way up to the big ones. Do not fret if there are some failures along the way. You did not learn to walk in one day either.

It also helps to make your manifesting exercises a priority in your life. Set aside meditation or concentration time every day and stick to it the same way you would a diet or exercise plan. Even though I know for a fact from being in the afterlife that I can and do manifest, I still have to make the daily effort to keep my focus on consciously manifesting. Remember, manifesting is way more than "imagining" something. If fantasizing worked, we would all be happy campers. Manifesting is literally creating physical reality. It takes a lot more commitment and effort than we may initially want to devote to it. Because it does take concentrated attention and intention, it is best to work on manifesting one life change at a time.

Technically, it only takes one focused attention and intention to manifest physical reality. But I find that being inside this body is so distracting that I personally have to focus my attention and intention over and over again. Force yourself to form a habit of turning your attention to what you want to manifest by putting reminder notes on your mirror, bedpost, refrigerator, computer, etc.

Generally speaking, when we are in the body we manifest in conformity with the existing collective manifestation of earth life. For example, if someone is not trim and muscular, he is not going to wake up one morning and find a body like Brad Pitt's staring back at him in the mirror. We Light Beings can, and do, perform miracles like that, but generally we avoid it. So manifesting a trim and muscular body will take the form of creating new opportunities to exercise and eat better. Maybe you will get a flyer in the mail about a gym opening up with a special introductory membership rate of $1 a month. That is your manifestation. Or a friend moves and gives you his exercise equipment. That is your manifestation. Or you hear about a drug that controls appetite and find out your insurance plan covers it. That is your manifestation. The human body still has to do the work to get into shape because of the biological nature of the human manifestation. What you will consciously manifest will be opportunities to get a trim and muscular body—if that fits with your spiritual purposes.

You cannot manifest wealth. Money is not going to fall from the sky into your hands, or mysteriously show up in your bank account, because that is not how the manifestation we call Earth is designed. Money has to come to you in a believable, though perhaps wonderful and surprising, way. Nor are you likely to manifest an entirely new wealthy lifestyle by just putting your attention and intention to it. Some manifestations require the cooperation of other Light Beings because the collective manifestation would have to be changed in order for your conscious manifestations to appear, thereby affecting many lives. Becoming wealthy is not a solo manifestation because it requires others to give you money. Your piece of the manifestation is to generate opportunities to make money by providing a service, selling something, winning a contest, or receiving a gift, grant, or inheritance. Then you actually have to perform the service, sell the item, enter the contest, or have a person in your life who could give you the gift (such as winning the Power Ball Lottery after buying lottery tickets). The person paying the money has to cooperate in your manifestation at both the soul and the Light Being level. When I want to manifest something that I know requires the agreement of other Light Beings, I say (call it a prayer if you like):

> To Source and all those Light Beings who might be affected: if it would be consistent with my mission and goals this life, I intend to change the manifestation of Nanci's life to ________. I ask that you focus your Energy with me to accomplish this and agree to change the collective manifestation to assist me.

Then I wait with the full expectation that something will happen. I may not know what, but I keep my eyes open so I will recognize my manifestation when it comes.

It is also possible that you have a hindering belief that is holding you back from bringing abundance into your life. Nothing will change in this regard until you find and change that belief.

You are holding on too tightly to what you have. It is human nature to want your cake and eat it too. For example, many men and women want to find another lover before terminating a marriage or relationship they already have. Or they want to find another job while they still have one. Or they want to continue taking drugs, drinking, overeating, or another destructive behavior while they try to change their beliefs to something healthier.

Another common problem is humans cling very tightly to what they have whether they actually want it or not. They are possessive and controlling by nature. Extreme cases are called hoarders. Milder examples include:

- keeping several lovers on a string because you cannot commit to one.

- keeping a deceased spouse's personal items or clothes because you cannot bear to part with them and think that having them is necessary to keep the memory of him/her alive.

- keeping closets full of clothes that no longer fit on the theory that someday you will get down to a weight that will allow you to wear them.

- keeping boxes of unread books or stacks of newspapers because you tell yourself you may want to read them someday.

- keeping a refrigerator and freezer full of food that has expired even though you rarely eat at home.

- a parent who keeps trying to run a child's life into adulthood.

- a patient who clings tightly to a diagnosis and makes it his/her identity.

- a person who gets so wrapped up in a job or career that it defines who they are even after retirement.

- a person who is wrapped so tightly trying to hold it all together that he/she cannot even relax his/her body's muscles.

You may have to let go of something you have now in order to manifest its replacement. For example, I was a person who held on to old beloved clothes because I kept telling myself that I would lose weight and be able to wear them again. In the meantime, I had taken to wearing sweats much of the time because they hide a multitude of sins (involving chocolate). After watching the TV show *What Not to Wear* several times, I decided I would give my entire business wardrobe away to a women's shelter and manifest clothes like the hosts of the TV show suggested. My friend and I delivered two carloads of clothes to the shelter. I threw away most of my grubby sweats. And I went to Macy's. In the past, I considered myself lucky to find one item that I liked and that fit me. On this trip, however, I was able to put together a decent wardrobe like the ones on the TV show—and the clothes were even on sale. I manifested an opportunity I had never experienced before, but only after I let go of what I was unreasonably clinging to.

You are caught in human resistance to change. The most common reason our conscious attempts to manifest something better into our lives fails is that we have not given up our old beliefs from which we manifest unconsciously. For example, I receive many emails from readers who ask essentially the same question as this one, though using different terms and scenarios:

> I meditate, and create the event in my mind's eye, and can clearly see the event in the mind dimension of the result I want to achieve. How do I pull that vision, or movie if you will, into my current reality?[89]

The reader who wrote this particular question informed me that he follows a technique called Quantum Jumping that he learned about on YouTube. He describes the technique as mentally viewing an event and then merging into it. Other readers have told me about various other quantum or law of attraction techniques they have tried without success. The reason this and other techniques do not work is because they do not reflect the truth about how Source manifests physical reality. This and other techniques I have read about are just plain human thinking, and are based on the core concept that something outside ourselves will give us what we want. So long as my reader, and all those following other techniques that are supposed to "pull" a mental vision into reality, continue to believe that they do not *create* their own lives, they will continue to fail to consciously manifest physical reality.

The bedrock belief that we are separate from Source is reflected in a lot of questions other readers ask. They have heard me mention the core entity Source and its various mental characters (us) and have latched on to that linguistic tool as an impediment to believing they cannot manifest on their own. They seem to be unable to get that separation partition idea out of their minds, as the previously referred to reader describes:

> Since the human animal part of us canNOT manifest physical reality, how can I directly link to my "inner Source" to be able to have inner Source communicate with "Main Source" to manifest the reality I am trying to create?[90]

This question discloses the two most difficult beliefs to change.

First, the reader cannot quite let go of the fact that he is not a human being, as indicated in his reference to the "human animal part of us." You must be able to accept that the physical body is an animal you inhabit as its soul, and that it is not a part of you in any way. It has a life of its own that you, the soul, can choose to influence or not. But it never was and never will be part of *you*. Second, it sounds like the reader believes that he, as human, has a soul that is not part of him, and therefore he has difficulty accessing it. He also thinks we souls are separate from Source and have to make supplication to "Main Source" for what we want. We cannot fault this reader in any way. This is the religious model we have all grown up believing. But continuing to believe it will hold us back from manifesting a happier life. You must believe that you *are* the soul part of the combined animal/soul being; that you *are* Source; and that because you are Source you can and do manifest the physical reality around you. If you cannot believe that, you will fail to form the requisite intention to consciously manifest because you will not believe you can do it.

Perhaps you have failed to identify these or other hindering beliefs because you do not want to self-examine or analyze your motivations or feel the emotions you know you have been stuffing for years. This is the normal human resistance to change and to the threat of feeling something that might end up being unpleasant. Ignore it. Work up the courage to face down whatever it is that has been causing you to manifest unhappy life experiences. I promise you it will not kill you. It will not cause permanent injury. Instead, it will start the healing process. And it will probably be far less painful than you imagine it will be. Humans feel much more fear anticipating pain than they do when they are actually subjected to pain and can see the end of it in sight.

Maybe you have identified the hidden belief that causes you to unconsciously manifest experiences you no longer want to have, but you resist changing your belief because it will result in changes in other people's lives. Fearing the effect changes in you will have on those around you is used as justification for refusing to change your belief. It sounds like an admirable reason. But it is an excuse rooted in the human animal need to control everything around it in order to protect itself from real and imaginary threats. You do not have the right to control other people's lives by failing to improve your own. You can go ahead and change your belief and automatically change your unconscious manifesting little by little. When you change your life, those around you are responsible for how they adapt to the change. You cannot control that, but they can. Give them the space to do so. The organization Al-Anon has a very effective program for how to deal with this particular issue that can help you if this is your sticking point. Most Al-Anon meetings welcome everyone, even those who may not have an alcoholic in their lives.

You are still following your law of attraction beliefs. I often get questions from readers who believe there is a law of attraction and who are trying to integrate what I have said about manifesting into that belief system. That will not work. The law of attraction and manifesting are opposite ends of the spectrum. The former says humans have the ability to attract bounty from an outside entity or the universe. The latter says we souls inside humans have the innate spiritual power as Source to literally create our own physical matter reality. Law of attraction theories are manmade. Manifesting is an eternal truth given to me by Source while I was in the afterlife. Manifesting, unlike law of attraction theory, requires nothing of the human body except silence of its thoughts. It does not depend upon our emotions at any given time, or upon our being "in the flow of the universe," or our thoughts, or our ability to visualize what we want. Manifesting plays no word games as it requires no words. Manifesting requires only our spiritual attention and intention to create physical reality.

Important Takeaways from Chapter 11

- You do not have to formally meditate in order to prepare your mind to consciously manifest, but you do have to concentrate solely on manifesting.
- You will not be able to predict how quickly your conscious manifestations will appear because there is no such thing as "time" in eternal life.
- If you feel discouraged, look for a hidden belief that might be standing in your way. Go back through the common hindering beliefs listed in Chapter 6 and see if one of them is the culprit. You may think you have changed a belief but unconsciously you are resisting the change.
- You can ask other Light Beings to add their co-creating attention and intentions to your own to help you manifest.
- You may not be able to change your life because you are holding on too tightly to what you already have. You have to be willing to let go, and to change and accept all the consequences change entails.

12

You Can Create a New Life

ONE OF MY READERS RECENTLY COMPLAINED TO me that he had read a lot of spiritual books and was still looking for something practical to improve his life—something that actually works.

Manifesting works. Everything in the universe is manifested.

Manifested reality is the only reality humans will ever know.

Manifesting is the only power capable of creating something out of nothing. Capable of creating physical matter. Capable of creating better events and opportunities in our lives. Capable of healing us. And capable of making us happier.

You hold the power of manifesting right within you. It is an innate ability you have as part of Source. You create your individual life as a distinct character within Source's mind. You do it consciously and unconsciously all the time without knowing it. You can choose to be the creator of your body's life too, instead of allowing him or her to run the show via animal instincts and drives. You can change your human experience through the spiritual power of manifesting.

Once you accept that you create your own life, you can begin to do it more consciously.

The only tool you need is your mind. You simply focus your mind as Source and concentrate your attention and intention on manifesting a change in your life.

The only work involved in manifesting is concentration. Paying attention. Focusing. All things you are used to doing in other contexts.

We Light Being souls create our individual lives in the exact same way Source manifested the entire universe. We do not automatically realize this because the amnesia that blankets our minds upon entering into the dense physical matter of a human body blocks our awareness of who and what we truly are. But we can unlock our memory. And remembering our ability to manifest reality allows us to use that power consciously, rather than unconsciously as we have been doing.

You can improve one aspect of your life by simply meditating and using that freedom from thoughts to consciously manifest an opportunity for change into your life. You can improve an entire course of experiences by identifying and correcting an old, musty, erroneous belief you have been unknowingly holding onto since childhood, and which you have been manifesting into your current life. Outdated beliefs have been holding you back from creating a happier life. But by changing them, you can heal the physical and emotional pain you have felt for years. You can be happy.

Make a promise to yourself now that you will try. That you will turn your attention and intention to one thing that you would like to improve in your life. That you will keep your eyes open and watch for and recognize your manifestation when it appears. It may come in the form of something you are inclined to call ironic, or a coincidence, fluke or good luck. It may take the form of something you interpret to be an omen.

Promise yourself that you will keep practicing until conscious manifesting becomes a habit.

You *can* manifest a new reality for yourself just by changing your mind as Source.

NOTES

Chapter 1

1. This book is addressed to the souls incarnated into human bodies. After the first four paragraphs of Chapter 1, when I use the word "we" or "us," I mean Source acting through its Light Being mental characters, including you and me, within the physical universe. I never refer to humans as "us" because I learned in the afterlife that the individuals we believe ourselves to be, the identities we recognize as ourselves, the personalities we believe belong to the bodies we inhabit, are actually the parts of Source's self-awareness that humans call "souls." We are the souls, not the bodies we inhabit.

2. The *Matrix* is a major motion picture starring Keanu Reeves, which was released five years after my 1994 visit to the afterlife. Its premise is that human-like robots have taken over the world and have turned humans into living batteries to produce the energy the robots need to operate. The humans are pacified with a movie of an idyllic Earth life projected directly into their minds.

All of my memories of how we and the universe were created are detailed in Chapters 2 and 3 of my third book, *Backwards Beliefs: Revealing Eternal Truths Hidden in Religions* (Columbus, OH: A.P. Lee & Co., 2011).

3. The casting of a veil of amnesia may at first sound like too foreign a concept to believe. Something in human experience that is a little similar to it is what psychologists used to call multiple personality disorder. In multiple personality disorder, a soul inside a human is so traumatized by life that it creates alternate personalities within itself, each of which believes it is real. The soul can do this because Source can do it and the soul is part of Source. Usually these alternate personalities

have no knowledge of their origin and no awareness of the other alternates. They are blanketed in amnesia.

Chapter 2

4. The answers I received to these questions form most of the content of *BACKWARDS: Returning to Our Source for Answers*, (Columbus, OH: A. P. Lee & Co., 2007); and *BACKWARDS Guidebook*, (Columbus, OH: A. P. Lee & Co., 2009).

5. This documentary vision of Earth history is detailed in my third book, *BACKWARDS Beliefs: Revealing Eternal Truths Hidden in Religions*, (Columbus, OH: A. P. Lee & Co., 2011).

6. Personal correspondence, Richard R. to Nanci Danison, December 15, 2016.

7. Natalie Sudman, *Application of Impossible Things: My Near Death Experience in Iraq* (Huntsville, AR: Ozark Mountain Publishing, 2012), 35.

8. This excerpt from Ms. Moorjani's account is taken from the Seattle IANDS Newsletter, posted on its website. The quotation is used with the written permission of the Seattle International Association for Near-Death Studies chapter and Author Anita Moorjani. See http://seattleiands.org/stories/Moorgani.htm for the full text of the account.

9. See http://near-death.com/experiences/notable/juliet-nightingale.html for the full text of the account.

10. See http://www.nderf.org/Experiences/1richard_l_nde.html for the full text of the account.

11. See http://www.nderf.org/Experiences/1mira_s_nde.html for the full text of the account.

12. See http://www.near-death.com/experiences/notable/Guenter-wagner.html for the full text of the account.

13. See http://www.near-death.com/experiences/notable/Christian-andreason.html for the full text of the account.

Chapter 3

14. There is an extensive discussion about what I learned in the afterlife about prayer in my book *Answers From The Afterlife*, (Columbus, OH: A.P. Lee & Co., 2016).

15. The purpose of life and how and why we set various goals for incarnation are described in detail in my books *BACKWARDS: Returning to Our Source for Answers, BACKWARDS Guidebook,* and *Answers From The Afterlife.*

Chapter 4

16. Rhonda Byrne, *The Secret* (New York: Atria Books, 2006).

17. Charles F. Haanel, *The Master Key System* (1916). You can download a free PDF version of the original correspondence course from http://www.masterkeysystem.com.

18. Ibid., Part 1, para. 25 combined with para. 26.

19. Ibid., Part 1, para. 29.

20. Ibid., Part 10, para. 11.

21. Ibid., Part 12, para. 22.

22. Ibid., Part 4, para. 6.

23. Ibid., Part 6, Introduction.

24. Ibid., Part 9, para. 25.

25. Ibid., Part 8, para. 18.

26. Byrne, *The Secret*, xii.

27. Napoleon Hill, *Think and Grow Rich!: The Original Version, Restored and*

Revised (Anderson, SC: Mindpower Press, 2015).

The original edition of *Think and Grow Rich!*, now out of print, was published in 1937. Ross Cornwell of Mindpower Press has reconstructed the original edition, editing out certain portions, changing some words, and annotating the result so that the reader will know what has been changed from the original. Hill admitted in correspondence to Charles Haanel that he relied in large part on *The Master Key System* for the content of *Think and Grow Rich!*. For example, Haanel originated Hill's statements that one's predominant mental attitude defines what manifests into physical reality and that like thoughts attract each other.

28. Ibid., Endnotes, chap. 2, n. 1.

29. Jerry Hicks refers to his and Ester Hicks's work as "teachings" and as a "philosophy," but not as eternal truths. Ester and Jerry Hicks, *Ask and It Is Given: Learning to Manifest Your Desires* (Carlsbad, CA: Hay House, 2004), xix.

30. Jerry Hicks discusses his introduction to and subsequent teaching of Hill's *Think and Grow Rich!* principles in the Preface to *The Astonishing Power of Emotions: Let Your Feelings Be Your Guide*, (Carlsbad, CA: Hay House, 2007).

31. Apparently Jerry Hicks had been using the 1960 edition of *Think and Grow Rich!*, which Napoleon Hill had revised from the 1937 edition to delete obsolete and outdated verbiage from the Great Depression era. Perhaps Hill intentionally deleted the word "vibration" because he no longer believed it appropriately described thoughts.

32. Haanel, *The Master Key System*, Part 21, para. 12.

33. Hill, 49.

34. Ibid., 50.

35. Hicks, *The Law of Attraction*, 32-33.

36. See, for example, Toshiaki Imada, Ph.D., "Brain Magnetic Fields (Magnetoencephalography: MEG)," December 22, 2004 (http://faculty.washington.edu/imada/brain.html). Dr. Imada is a Research Professor at the University of Washington Department of Speech and Hearing Sciences and Technical Director

of the I-LABS MEG Brain Imaging Center.

In the 1980s, I volunteered to be a test subject in a study conducted by a graduate student in physics at Ohio State University. The study was designed to measure the strength of the brain's magnetic field outside the skull. The first meeting of volunteers ended in so much chaos that the grad student sent us all home without enrolling any of us in the study. He could not even explain the test parameters to the group of volunteers because so many of them were shouting at him that everyone already knows that thoughts are magnetic!

37. Ibid., 2.

38. Hill, *Think and Grow Rich!*, 47.

39. Ibid., 44.

40. Hicks, *Ask and It Is Given*, 22.

41. Ibid., 310.

42. This concept is included in the material posted on the Seth website, http://sethlearningcenter.org.

43. Hicks, *The Law of Attraction*, 9-12.

44. Hicks, *Ask and It Is Given*, xxii-xxiv.

Chapter 5

45. Haanel, *The Master Key System*, Part 17, para. 6.

46. Byrne, *The Secret*, 38–39.

47. I am not advocating that everyone follow every urge he/she feels. Most urges are generated by the body, not the soul, and relate to pleasure seeking or other animal drives, not spiritual goal fulfillment.

48. Haanel, Part 16, para. 1.

49. Personal correspondence, Gary M. to Nanci Danison, January 9, 2016.

50. Eckhart Tolle, *The Power of Now: A Guide to Spiritual Enlightenment* (Novato, CA: New World Library/Namaste Publishing, 1999).

Chapter 6

51. Hill, *Think and Grow Rich!*, 17, 29.

52. I, on the other hand, did not manifest in heaven anything even remotely similar to the Catholic beliefs about the afterlife or my place in it. However, when I was testing whether or not I was the one creating the physical environments I saw, I did manifest an extremely real railroad trestle tunnel, sunny meadow, and hospital corridor. I realized at the time that I was creating those earth-like scenes with my thoughts because I expected to see them.

53. Spencer Johnson, MD, *Who Moved My Cheese?: An A-Mazing Way to Deal with Change in Your Work and in Your Life* (New York: G. P. Putnam's Sons, 2002).

54. Eugene T. Gendlin, PhD, *Focusing*, (rev. ed.) (New York: Bantam Books, 1981); Michael Brown, *The Presence Process: A Healing Journey into Present Moment Awareness* (New York: Beauford Books, 2005).

55. I have seen various scientific papers that attribute all thoughts, emotions, beliefs, memories, skills, etc., to the human unconscious and/or subconscious levels of awareness. This is understandable because scientists are generally not willing to acknowledge and accept that we souls exist, have incarnated into humans, and have our own minds, memories, and levels of awareness. But I learned in the afterlife that most of what scientists attribute to the human mind is actually part of the Light Being mind.

56. Personal correspondence, Ralph K. to Nanci Danison, May 30, 2015.

57. The TLC channel show called *My 600-lb Life* features patients who weigh over 600 pounds who are receiving medical treatment for weight loss, part of which involves the physician emphasizing the risk of death. Only rarely does a patient's morbidly obese spouse, parents, siblings, or children change their eating habits despite what they learn being on the show. They simply deny to themselves

that they too are morbidly obese because they do not weigh 600 pounds.

Chapter 7

58. Personal correspondence, Tom T. to Nanci Danison, February 12, 2013.

59. Personal correspondence, Tuula B. to Nanci Danison, March 28, 2013.

60. Personal correspondence, Catherine W. to Nanci Danison, July 15, 2013.

61. Ibid.

62. Personal correspondence, Jean-Pierre D. to Nanci Danison, December 5, 2012.

63. Personal correspondence, Robert R. to Nanci Danison, November 24, 2010.

64. Personal correspondence, Mary Ann K. to Nanci Danison, June 21, 2013.

65. Personal correspondence, Randy K. to Nanci Danison, February 14, 2014.

66. Personal correspondence, Stephanie P. to Nanci Danison, October 22, 2012.

Chapter 8

67. Mary C. Neal, MD, *To Heaven and Back* (Colorado Springs, CO: Waterbrook Press, 2012), xi–xii.

68. Byrne, *The Secret*, 14.

69. Hill, *Think And Grow Rich!*, 47.

70. Hicks, *Ask and It Is Given*, 26.

Chapter 9

71. Personal correspondence, Writer's Identity Withheld to Nanci Danison, February 2, 2016.

72. Ibid.

Chapter 10

73. National Institutes of Health, "Stem Cell Basics I," http:\\stemcells.nih.gov/info/basics/1.htm.

74. Clair Davies, NCTMB, and Amber Davies, NCTMB, *The Trigger Point Therapy Workbook: Your Self-Treatment Guide for Pain Relief,* 2nd ed. (Oakland, CA: New Harbinger Publications, 2004). This workbook is based on the leading medical text by Janet Travell, MD, and David Simons, MD, *Myofascial Pain and Dysfunction: The Trigger Point Manual* 2nd ed. (Baltimore, MD: Williams & Wilkins, 1999).

75. Alexander Loyd, PhD, ND, and Ben Johnson, MD, DO, NMD, *The Healing Code* (New York: Grand Central Life & Style, 2010).

76. Candace B. Pert, PhD, *Molecules of Emotion: The Science Behind Mind-Body Medicine* (New York: Scribner, 1997).

77. This is not my original idea. It is a paraphrasing of a meditation my sister's friend taught me.

78. Danison, *BACKWARDS: Returning to Our Source for Answers*, 156-157.

79. Candace B. Pert, PhD, was an internationally recognized neuroscientist and pharmacologist who discovered the opiate receptor on cells. This and other discoveries made her a major contributor to Mind-Body Medicine research.

80. Pert, *Molecules of Emotion*, 143.

81. Ibid., 141, 243.

82. NDEr and NDE researcher P.M.H. Atwater has stated in various forums

that it takes an average of seven years for an NDEr to process the event, emotions, and life changes the near-death experience produces.

83. Eugene T. Gendlin, PhD, *Focusing,* rev. ed. (New York: Bantam Books, 1981). I also recommend Ann Weiser Cornell, PhD, *The Power of Focusing: A Practical Guide to Emotional Self-Healing* (New York: MJF Books 1996). Dr. Cornell studied under Dr. Gendlin and taught at his institute.

84. Peter A. Levine, PhD, and Ann Frederick, *Waking the Tiger: Healing Trauma* (Berkeley, CA: North Atlantic Books, 1997).

85. Diane Poole Heller, PhD, and Laurence S. Heller, PhD, *Crash Course: A Self-Healing Guide to Auto Accident Trauma & Recovery* (Berkeley, CA: North Atlantic Books, 2001).

86. Ibid., 13.

87. Michael Brown, *The Presence Process: A Healing Journey into Present Moment Awareness* (New York: Beauford Books, 2005).

88. Jon Kabat-Zinn, PhD, *Full Catastrophe Living: Using the Wisdom of Your Body and Mind to Face Stress, Pain, and Illness*, rev. ed. (New York: Bantam Books, 1990, 2013).

Chapter 11

89. Personal correspondence, L. A. to Nanci Danison, July 7, 2017.

90. Ibid., October 31, 2017.

About the Author

UNTIL MARCH 1994, NANCI L. DANISON, ESQ. LIVED the life of a successful trial lawyer with a national reputation as a health lawyer practicing as a partner in a large, prestigious, multi-city Midwestern law firm. Then, she died during an invasive radiological procedure before breast cancer surgery, plunging her further into the afterlife than previously thought survivable. She returned to share her memories of what she learned in heaven.

Nanci was a National Merit Finalist in Catholic high school where she graduated magna cum laude. She earned a Bachelor of Science degree in biology (anatomy and physiology major) and chemistry magna cum laude, a Bachelor of Arts degree in psychology magna cum laude, and a doctorate in jurisprudence. She has been listed in *Who's Who* and has for decades been counted among the top five percent of lawyers in America for skill and ethics in Martindale-Hubbell's *Bar Register of Preeminent Lawyers.*

Visit www.BackwardsBooks.com for more information about Nanci's previous four books on her memories from the afterlife.